Co-senior: Sweetheart, do you have problems remembering to charge your phone?
Me: Yes.
Co-senior: Then I'm not buying you a Tesla.

Dedicated to Co-Senior,
The love of my life
who charges all my batteries.

There is *Life After Retirement*
Find Your *Purpose* and *Laugh Out Loud*

I'M NOW CALLED A SENIOR

Stories from the *Heart*

JULIE SURSOK

Lifechange Productions Pty Ltd
P.O. Box 563,
St Ives
NSW 2075

I'M NOW CALLED A SENIOR - STORIES FROM THE HEART

ISBN: 978-0-6487598-4-3 (Paperback)
ISBN: 978-0-6487598-5-0 (ebook)

Thank you for buying my book
I would love to give you *THE DOWNSIZING STEP BY STEP WORKBOOK*

100% free

TO DOWNLOAD GO TO:

https://imnowcalledasenior.com/downsizingplanner

Contents

Preface

"JULE, JULE, QUICKLY, COME!" MY SISTER FRANTICALLY yells from the bed next to mine in our family's holiday home.

I am accustomed to her calling out at this time of night. She has hurt her back playing tennis, and I dutifully jump out of bed to turn her over.

This time, however, it is different.

I open my eyes and freeze. Standing on my bed, two storeys up, a huge figure looms over me in the shadows, holding a torch covered by a red cloth.

One foot is on the windowsill and one foot on my bed.

My scream is blood curdling. It wakes my parents in their bedroom next door. My dad comes running through with a golf club in his hand.

"*Thud*," the intruder jumps from the window to the ground far below and limps off.

He is eventually captured.

It is the start of a very challenging year.

It is the year I lost a year of school.

I am eight.

How does a surgeon's daughter manage to have her tonsils removed, her burst appendix extracted, contract encephalitis followed by jaundice, poke her finger in a wall plug and fly across a room, and finally, experience an anaphylactic reaction to a sulfur antibiotic—all in one year?

There is, however, a good side to this story.

I gain a year of reading.

Books become my beloved companion, healing my brain and abject loneliness.

My contemporaries are living their little-girl dreams in a froth of Barbies and friendships. I am locked in a dream of isolation, immersed in the stories of other little girl's lives.

I read a book a day.

The librarian complains that I can read books far more advanced than my age but probably wouldn't understand the words nor the teenage insinuations.

Who would have thought that *that* time would provide the spark and the tools that would propel me at such high velocity to what I really love to do at the other end of life?

It takes guts to be a sick little girl and still be positive on the other side. It takes guts to start an author's career on the other side. But I have done it, and so can you.

What was your spark way back then? What were the skills you were collecting when you didn't know why?

These tools are waiting for you under this mangled mess of life, and they will show themselves gloriously to you one day.

Run as fast as you can towards the light, grab and hold tight, grow and learn. Keep close to your heart.

Here are my stories, from then and now, stories from the heart.

I hope you relate and enjoy.

They may inspire you to go out there and write your own story.

It's your turn now.

> The power to inspire is rare. Moments like this are rare. You think you may not be ready, that you'll do it at a more convenient time. But you don't choose the time. The time chooses you. Either you seize what may turn out to be the only chance you have, or you decide you're willing to live with the knowledge that the chance has passed you by.
>
> – *Teddy Kennedy to Barack Obama*

Relax Seniors—You Are Allowed To

TODAY IS THE FIRST DAY OF OUR "ISOLATION" HOLIDAY, and co-senior is going nuts. He can't sit still.

He is racing around the house as if it hasn't been looked after for a zillion years.

The washing is done, lawn is mowed, dishes are immaculate, dust is destroyed, and he is still going.

I should be grateful, I know, as it means I don't have to drag myself off my chaise lounge and tear myself away from my latest gossip magazine to even think about it. But I can't catch co-senior. He is lost in a flurry of "to do". The minute business deadlines were no longer, it seems that there are now house deadlines that need to be met.

"Hon, pretend we are in a holiday house the next two weeks," I implore gently.

"Forget about all the surrounding stuff, it's time now to have some fun. We are on holiday!"

"But all the housework needs to be done," he retorts, as if I hadn't been hands-on for the past year. "Look, the lawn needs further mowing, the gutters need cleaning, the fridge needs emptying."

"I know," I exclaim in exasperation, "but the only cleaning the fridge is going to get is from the indulgence of the Christmas leftovers, and then it will be ship-shape."

I try to be funny.

Co-senior stares at me blankly.

"Attachment to your hobbies is for *this* time. We are on holiday. Stop this whirlwind of action! Go to gym, wear yourself out, and in the meantime, I will make myself busy by calling food home delivery with our meals for tomorrow. And, oh, by the way, pick up a bottle of wine on the way home."

I think co-senior is registering. He is usually very compliant with Queen Bee's suggestions. I think he is looking for his gym gear as he is very quiet.

I find him, however, sitting on the cold garage floor with the vacuum cleaner upturned, patiently unpicking threads of dental floss that have somehow floated into the roller and have now seized up the entire piece of equipment. I am secretly quite glad. This means he doesn't have the right tools, so no more lifting my legs as I type while he manoeuvres into all the corners around my desk.

I now need to go on a search mission to find his gym compression pants, as he seems to be very involved. I can't find them, as there is much "lost property" also going on in the house. Pants are mixed up with pillow slips, and nighties are mixed up with towels. Co-senior has taken it upon himself to be Head of Laundry. This is a new duty he has found, so I am ready for a few novice slip-ups.

"Sweetheart, are you going to the gym? What time does it shut?"

No reply.

"*Sweetheart*. . . . Are you going to the gym?"

Still no reply.

"Are you going to gym?" I now shout out in a more strident tone, as I pace up and down the loungeroom.

As I glance outside, I see co-senior lying on the chaise lounge that I have recently vacated. He has his *Economist* held up and his swimming gear on, and I breathe a sigh of relief. At last, I don't have to check out the Airbnbs in the beach area to force this whirlwind to slow down.

A brief thought does, however, flit through my mind. As I was looking at the calorie value of the sourdough bread I have been buying recently, I notice that there is an iodine ingredient added. Iodine!!! Maybe his thyroid has gone "ball-oo-gas". This surely is the reason for this manic continuous movement?

I dismiss this notion as quickly as it arises. Surely if his thyroid is racing gangbusters, mine would be too, but I am not seeing any "Busy Bee" side effects.

I tiptoe upstairs so as not to disturb him, cursing myself as I spill coffee on the carpet, as I know this will trigger a cleaning frenzy.

As I sit down to write another chapter, I hear rustling downstairs.

"Is that you, darl? Why are you back inside?"

"The buggers just go for me. They just go for me!"

I sigh and walk downstairs.

Co-senior is now togged up in full protection gear with coloured bangles of anti-mosquito deterrent hanging off anything that can be attached. He looks miserable.

I grab a bucket and a cloth and hand it over.

"I spilled my coffee on the carpet."

His face lights up, and his trigger is activated. He gets to work with a smile on his face. While rubbing and de-staining, he simply doesn't have to think. He has his earbuds in his ears jiggling to Taylor Swift's "Shake It Off".

Today this is his holiday happy. It will change tomorrow—whatever blows his hair back, whatever he has left.

This is his form of relaxation.

We are all different.

I claim back my chaise lounge, quite happy in my own relaxation space. It is a welcome relief after an oddly busy year.

You relax too, seniors. Find your very own relaxation space, especially when it is safer to be at home at the moment.

There will be many rewards.

You know you actually **are allowed to.**

JUST A THOUGHT

"Take a deep breath, inhale peace, exhale happiness."

– A. D. Posey

SENIOR SAGE

If you never stop, you never regroup, rewire and regenerate. You spin out of control and eventually spin out of energy—so find your relaxation space and submit. You can give yourself permission, you know.

Lose Control to Have Control

I AM AWAY INTERSTATE ON BUSINESS, KEEPING A close eye on the Flightradar24 app as I wade through some necessary paperwork.

It's a thing when you are a frightened flyer and your daughter is about to board a plane to fly across the ocean to foreign lands. You become adept at aircraft type and wingspan and load and weather and everything that describes flight. It is part exhilarating and part terrifying.

My flying anxiety has shamefully rubbed off onto my daughter. She also now looks at her watch during flight one hundred million times and goes to the bathroom one hundred million times and is terrorised by bumps and drops and noises. It is going to take a long time to extricate her fear from mine, and I feel guilty.

"Fly safe, darling. Text when you land. Love you" is my last communication before the cabin door is closed.

I settle back into paperwork, imagining her sipping champagne to dull the nerves, encased by noise-cancelling earphones and engrossed in the latest entertainment offering.

Glancing over to my computer, I see the blue plane ascent line is moving, and she is up and rising rapidly to her cruising altitude.

She is on her way.

Figures are completed, and paperwork is ready for the next day.

I indulge in a long shower, ready for a few chapters and sleep.

I glance back at the screen and freeze.

The blue line is no longer moving up, it is plummeting down. This is in the middle of the ocean.

My entire body screams fear.

I call co-senior.

"The *pppplane* is going down!"

"What are you talking about?" answers co-senior calmly.

"I am following the flight on Flightradar24, and the lines are moving in the wrong direction. Is she landing anywhere on the way? Did she tell you about a stop along the way? What is going on? I am freaking out!"

Co-senior reassures me.

"Relax now, it is just technology. Remember the time the radar showed us circling and landing nowhere? It happens. Breathe, and go to sleep. You are just neurotic about flying. All will be fine."

Breathe and go to sleep—OK, right.

I am glued to the screen, adrenaline pumping. My body shakes and I am transfixed.

And then the plane is at zero.

ZERO!!!!

Where is she?

Where is ZERO!!!!?

WHERE IS MY GIRL?

I call her phone -and nothing.

I wait and call her phone—and nothing. I wait and wait and call her phone and still nothing.

I sink to the floor, my heart exploding, my body collapsing.

And then the phone rings. Her number lights up the screen.

"Mum."

"Where the hell are you? What has happened? Oh, thank God, you are ok!"

"Mum, listen, we have made an emergency landing on the tip of Canada. The plane lost electrical power. The Captain managed to turn around and land at an air force base in Stephenville."

Her voice is shaky. She is shaken.

I am shaky.

She is on the ground.

She tells me that passengers were so quiet as they held their breath on landing in this extremely remote part of the world. When a replacement aircraft arrived, the new Captain remarked that he was astounded that the former Captain had been able to do what he had done.

We were lucky that day.

It was her birthday.

♥

Christmas and holidays work hand in hand.

This same daughter is excited. She is off to Thailand for a summer holiday, and she is counting down the days.

We wave good-bye.

"Fly safe, my darling! Text when you get there. Love you."

The plane disappears into the blue expanse, and we drive home.

"Eagle has landed, great flight—about to board to Phuket,"

Half the flying is done; we can half relax.

It is Boxing Day, and we celebrate at a friend's annual Boxing Day leftover party. I know it's a leftover party as my Mum's birthday was on Boxing Day. Her birthday celebration was always peppered somewhere with cold cuts and Christmas pudding.

I am still unsettled.

I know it is the subconscious "my daughter is in the sky somewhere" fear.

I endeavour to slap it down as fast as it raises its ugly head.

The lunch is going well, but it is well past the landing time—and nothing!!!

With an inconspicuous trip to the bathroom, phone in hand, I Google-search flight weather. All is just fine.

Returning to the table I pour myself another comforting glass of wine.

I am not enjoying myself and coerce co-senior to go home to become a parental flight investigator. He is not that happy as he has found a new friend and they are digging deep into the highs and lows of the share market.

The host is not happy and never invites us again to her annual occasion.

We return home, and in my mellowed state I start "surfing." Nothing screams danger.

But, there has been an earthquake in Sumatra.

I am ignorant. Where is Sumatra? I discover that Sumatra is in the same vicinity as Phuket. I am starting to feel uncomfortable.

The flight time is one hour and twenty-five minutes. I had checked that—I know everything about flight times, arrivals and departures. I would be a star as a new intern on the information desk for our national airline.

Six hours have lapsed.

The phone rings - her number!

"Mum, I am in Bangkok."

Bangkok? She left Bangkok hours ago.

"The flight was delayed on takeoff, and I was doing so well. We were approaching Phuket, landing gear was out, it was a beautiful sunny day without a cloud in the sky, and then suddenly we were going up again!"

"Mum, I was so scared." Her voice desperately quivers.

I change to soothing Mum mode.

"Sweetheart, are you okay? What happened? What did the pilot say? What went wrong?"

"Mum, there was no explanation for such a long time. The air crew looked so confused. We were all confused. I'm scared, Mum!"

An earthquake that is thought to have had the energy of twenty-three thousand Hiroshima-type atomic bombs occurred in the Indian Ocean, and a massive tsunami ensued. The pilot saw the water approaching seconds before landing and aborted. If the plane had been on time, it would have been a different story.

It was Boxing Day.

Europe isn't far from Africa when you live in Africa.

We would save hard for a flight across the continent to experience new worlds and new cultures and new ideas.

The situation in Africa, however, had become trickier. Sanctions applied, forcing change of an inhumane government enforced system. Flights no longer flew direct to their destination but were required to deviate around the bulge of Africa. Nobody wanted to make life easy for a country that allowed such an unequal existence.

Our saving budget is reached, and we are off and away with two children in tow. The flight is going famously, and the flight attendant is preparing the evening meal.

The dinner-and-drinks trolley is jammed in the aisle next to our row. There is no possibility of a quick exit.

And then we are falling. We are falling at breakneck speed.

The flight attendant dives to the floor.

"What is happening?" we ask.

"I don't know. This has never happened before."

The plane tilts on its side, falling, falling, falling. I am so very frightened.

With an ear-blasting roar, someone or something is endeavouring to straighten up the situation.

"Oh, God, please keep us safe. Oh, God, please keep us safe," we pray loudly.

The plane rectifies its pitch, and we are straight once again. Both we and our drinks are shaken and stirred.

The plane had hit a wind shear—a Saharan Desert changeover to Gulf of Guinea wind shear—and we had shared the experience. It wasn't nice.

An aircraft full of passengers had succumbed to this same phenomenon in that area years before, and no one lived to tell the tale. We could have been the second victims.

We were the lucky ones.

♥

Our flight is ready for boarding. We are emigrating to a foreign land, and we are all nervous and excited.

As we are about to board,

"*Ding dong,*"

"Will all passengers travelling on Air Mauritius present at the check-in counter?"

"We may have been upgraded," I wink hopefully at co-senior.

Not to be. The aircraft has mechanical problems, and we are delayed.

The airline staff issue us with dining vouchers and free lounge access. We retreat to the departure lounge to hug our family a little longer, all red-eyed and sad.

Eventually we board in a flurry of good-byes and are on our way to our new life adventure—co-senior, me, and two tired and clingy little ones.

We arrive safely, check into our hotel, and collapse. It has been an emotional day.

There is a bevy of bustle outside our bedroom door.

"Have you seen? Have you seen?" the room attendant exclaims, flapping the *Mauritius Times* in our faces. "It is one of yours."

Screaming out at us in bold and enlarged type is the headline: **"Jumbo jet goes down in Mauritius."**

This was at the exact time of our landing in Mauritius—just by another aircraft.

Our parents are frantic. We have no mobile devices and flick through hotel information folders to work out how to dial out. "Hi, Mum and Dad. The eagle has landed. We are safe."

We all cry.

On 28 November 1987, a Boeing 747 Combi named *Helderberg* experienced a catastrophic in-flight fire in the cargo area, broke up in mid-air, and crashed into the Indian Ocean east of Mauritius, killing all 159 people on board.

And then we lost an engine over the Indian Ocean and limped erratically back to land.

And then my cousin, a pilot, died on his honeymoon with a joystick in his hand.

And then my friend's nephew came down in Malaysia Airlines MH17

And…

I hope I haven't scared you off. I shouldn't have. I should have given you bold courage.

I am still here, am I not?

No wonder I was the first candidate to join the Fearless Flyer's Course, and no wonder my passion of being a flight attendant is no longer pricking at my "I want to accomplish" list.

It's quite fine to change course.

We have no control when the doctor operates.

We have no control when the bus driver drives.

We have no control when we depart this life.

We have no control when the pilot flies.

Your gut will steer you in the right direction to make the right choices, and then it is time to let go, to lose control.

You will gain it back so calmly when you understand that when we submit, we are free of fear.

We will gain so much more of life when we release the bondage.

Lose control to have control.

If you love to travel, you have to fly.

So trust that the system has worked it all out and we will always text to our loved ones, "The eagle has landed."

JUST A THOUGHT

"Incredible change happens in your life when you decide to take control of what you do have power over instead of craving control over what you don't."

– Steve Maraboli, Life, the Truth, and Being Free

SENIOR SAGE

Some of us fear loosening the security of control. We fear not being able to deal with the results. If we try to control all in our life path, we will never live. So, give it a try. I guess freedom and more fun is on the other side.

When Did You Last...?

WHEN DID YOU LAST SIT IN THE CAR AFTER A GROCERY shop and pick the chocolate chips out of the muffin six-pack you bought for co-senior and the grandkids' visit?

I did just that today.

Somehow, my mouth went rogue from mask-protection release.

At first call, I felt rather guilty and then I didn't, as the sugar excess steered me into sugar-overload comatose and I was so hazy I no longer cared. And...the double-choc, gluten-free muffin tear-apart was memorable. I can still feel the taste of "more."

So, when did you last do stuff like that?

When did you last walk into the ocean and feel the icy water lapping over your feet and squelch the wet sand between your toes?

When did you throw a ball for a dog into that same water and dance in circles as the sprays of water shake from its fur?

When did you last laugh, collapse laugh and cry laugh and feel that inward, deep, belly laugh? Does that seem so far back in the memory bank, or can you still feel it?

When did you last sit in a cosy corner, read a book, and get lost in the imagination and colours of an innovative story or the life of a person who has so much to tell?

When did you last sit with a senior and listen to their stories and experiences that can only enrich and enhance your future? When did you last realise you may be the only person who is still listening?

When did you last tell someone that you loved them—really loved them—and experience the joy of giving back rather than receiving?

When did you last pray to the one you believe in? When did you last tell them you are hurting or worrying or sharing or simply OK?

When did you last call a friend and say that you love them, even though it may seem awkward and unusual?

When did you last see the homeless in their destitution and give them your second guitar or a hot coffee or whatever lies at the bottom of your coin purse?

When did you last see a kookaburra, sitting on the sawn-off branch outside your bedroom window, hoping for the crumbs from your latest snack?

When did you last throw snowballs or throw Frisbees or swim underwater or experience new countries or wonder at the creatures that live in the sky and in the sea and in tiny burrows?

When did you last have a full heart and not a full pocket?

When did you last say thank you to all those who help others?

Maybe it's time, dear seniors, to feel these emotions again. We are alive. We are lucky to be alive.

When did you last say, “I am truly grateful that I am still waking up every day and am ready to immerse myself in this glorious story of life”?

Your attitude will always determine your altitude—it is now your time to soar.

JUST A THOUGHT

"Tell me, princess, now when did you last let your heart decide?"

– Aladdin

SENIOR SAGE

It's time to remember what makes you happy and create the answer today to "When did you last?"

Just Laugh at Yourself

CO-SENIOR AND I HAVE THIS THING GOING.

I loathe to book my weekly lymphatic massage because of the current situation. The notion of hands all over me that may have touched some unknown spreader doesn't work for a germaphobe.

Pivot is a recent addition to our vocabulary. We are learning a new "viral" vocabulary, which we practice fervently in our senior homeschooling, pandemic-protection world. In this search for viral higher education, we are most diligent, and download several video tutorials on how to approach these medically necessary procedures.

We are very committed "later age" students, albeit rather ambitious, and watch each body-section lecture on repeat to ensure we have fully absorbed the content without referring to our copious notes in copious mislaid notebooks.

We've got this.

I climb onto our newly bought massage table, place my face in the face hole for better breathing, and stare at a well-worn carpet, a vagrant mosquito, and co-senior's mismatched socks.

I am, of course, in the "nuddies," and co-senior has lovingly placed a heater right next to my posterior, which is now glowing like the sun in its efflorescence. Actually, *effleurage* is one of the terms of my so-called massage, so maybe it all got a little mixed up.

And then Madame raises her head.

Co-senior is really trying his best. He is, however, forgetting the progressive routine, and it is creating a cesspool of intense irritation. The minute he moves out of sequence, I become the diligent taskmaster. Co-senior doesn't know that I have refreshed my memory on numerous occasions, as in pure honesty, I was forgetting it all myself.

So Bossy Bertha starts chirping.

"You go this way, not that. You don't slide, you pull. Not too hard; it hurts. Not too soft; it doesn't work. You start at the top and not the bottom. Your hands are too cold. Your hands are too warm. The heater is too hot; it's burning my bum. The heater is too cold; it's freezing my tits. I can't breathe face down as we haven't vacuumed. I want to just lie; I don't want to talk."

And so it continues.

Co-senior good naturedly switches off. He would much rather be having a long hot shower and reading a chapter of his latest book. But he now has to listen to this incessant pecking from an impatient serial provoker. He starts singing "Patience Is a Virus."

This makes me narkier in his attempt to be funny.

And then the comeback, and good on him.

"I wonder how much I would get for you if I sold you to a butcher? I would probably make a fortune."

And we both collapse in floods of laughter.

JUST A THOUGHT

"Impatient people, according to Bacon, are like the bees, and kill themselves in stinging others."

– Georgie Eliot

SENIOR SAGE

As we grow older, we seem to become more patient yet more impatient. Maybe we should take a little break between what we feel and what we say, and all will be good in the hood.

The Favourite Gagga and Pappa

"LET'S CHOOSE THE HOTTEST DAY NEXT WEEK AND GO to the beach."

This is music to my ears.

I was born in Johannesburg—dry, dusty, inland Johannesburg. A trip to the sea was wrapped in excitement, and we couldn't wait to spend our holiday time running in and out of the waves.

And now we live next to the sea (affirmations do work). "Hat, check. Sunscreen, check. Towels, check. Bag, check. Magazine, check. Sunglasses, check." Ready, set, go!

As the sand squelches between our toes, we know it is going to be a beautiful day.

It is very busy on the beach, a national holiday. The sun beckons all—some who have travelled farther than far to be there. We are all social distancing.

There are bodies everywhere in various stages of undress.

We spoil ourselves and hire a chair and umbrella and carve our little piece of heaven just far enough from the rising tide and just near enough to drop the costume wrap to run into the sea. Limited body exposure is needed as the elastic in my swimming costume has waved good-bye and my body bits are readjusting to find coverage without poking out a little extra.

The weather is warm, and we can't wait for a little vitamin D top up before running into the ocean.

"Excuse me!"

We look up.

"Would it be possible to look after our bags for us while we go for a swim?"

Well, we had just arrived, so that would work, I suppose.....

Off the bikini beauties run, and we glance at each other hoping that something unexpected or contagious isn't now hiding under our chair.

"Excuse me."

We look up again.

A bunch of hunky teenage males have approached while our noses are buried in page 1 of our magazine.

"Can we leave our bags with you?"

Um, second group. Do we emit some sort of pheromone that is attracting young nubiles to approach and retreat?

"Yeh," we say more hesitantly this time as the space under our chaise lounge is now getting crowded, and the bags are not adhering to social distancing rules.

I raise my eyebrows and look at co-senior. "Why us?"

We slink down a little lower, bunkering down into the latest magazine article on reality show scandal. We want to be unnoticed.

"Can I leave my bag here?" Another group of touristy-looking bodies approaches.

I turn to co-senior. "Have we become the beach locker room?"

We are now surrounded by bags of every colour, pattern, style, and description. There are so many bags in our circle of trust that we can't climb off our "chaisies."

We are now hot.

"Can we leave them here and go for a swim?"

Co-senior nods his head. He is very reliable. There may be passports in the bags or asthma puffers or who knows what, and if we leave, there sure as nuts could be some fast fingers and us goody, goody seniors will be laid to blame.

We are now hotter.

We can't see the bag owners in the sea, mainly because we have brought our old glasses in case our new pairs are scratched in the sand.

We can't leave for fear of reprisal.

We are stuck, sweaty, sticky, trapped, and irritated.

We have, however, earned an award, and we will accept this. We are the number one favourite "bagsitter" on the beach.

We are safe and reliable and look old, so that must mean honest.

We are the security attaché for young peoples' bags and possessions.

We are today's favourite Gagga and Pappa.

Next time, we will invite a friend to accompany us to the beach. We met him on a cruise, singing karaoke duets in the vodka bar.

He is a walking artform and wears lots and lots of studs and piercings to appear to be tough and badass. He also happens to be monstrously tall and monstrously big. We will hire him his very own "chaise" and umbrella and place him right between us, one and a half metres apart, with his very own copy of *Rolling Stone*. This is a stereotype misbehave, I know.

But we will pretend that it matters this time so we can at least bob around in the ocean, and nobody, yes, nobody will endeavour or even think of "approach and deposit."

JUST A THOUGHT

"Reliability is the precondition for trust."

– Wolfgang Shauble

SENIOR SAGE

Never over promise and under deliver. Rather, under promise and over deliver. It makes the recipient so much happier.

Apoocollapse

It is an early start in the senior's household this morning. It seems that Australia has gone "potty" in its sprint to the closest supermarket to secure anything that would suffice for a sparkling clean derriere.

In our household, we are down to the last square, and it has now become a severe degree of necessity, but it seems that the present-day coronavirus epidemic has been misinterpreted as "colon-a-virus," and dribbling noses and coughs replace dribbling bums and farts.

We are generally well-behaved, patient little queuers in suburbia, generous of spirit in waiting our turn. But this mass panic stampede for this vital acquisition is certainly bringing out the hidden little devils way deep down in our "prepper's" psyche.

Co-senior thinks five thirty a.m. will surely bring positive results but starts to wane in his expectation when he encounters a "sunrise" crowd jostling for position in front of the supermarket security gate. At first movement of security gate ascent, bodies fall prostrate to hold position and then orientation begins to find the aisle that will secure them first place in the toilet roll acquisition race.

Much to their dismay, security sentinels at the end of the aisle are enjoying their superiority, gleefully handing out rations to impatient hunters and gatherers.

Co-senior manages to get a pack, albeit not my bamboo, no dye, recycled, vegan, gluten-free variety. Co-senior is well versed in the manufacturing additives and knows that if he looks for something sans everything, he will be hero of the day.

I am overjoyed as I grab my book ready for a "shit in," but I am still fixated on an element of anxiety that this pack will not last forever and there will be a whole repeat episode to obtain next week's ration.

So, in my meditation during "sit in", I am well prepared to breathe in and breathe out and focus on joy and calm and health and gratification, but all I can think of is how thick the old telephone directory is and how long it will take to be used up in its conversion to toilet paper.

Will I choose a letter of the alphabet in the book where addresses of friends who had hurt were located, enjoying our association coming to a smelly end swirling away to oblivion?

I read I could use corncobs, but they are strategically bought as a side to a new dish this week and they are also organic and extremely hard to find, so I won't subject them to ignominy.

There has also been a deluge of rain for the past few weeks, and vegetation is blossoming, so maybe the large green leaves on a plant that I can't identify is the go. But when I search on Google, it looks like a poison ivy variety. I have a new general practitioner, and I don't think I would be too comfortable fronting up at his emergency after-hours with a searing posterior. I know me—I would wait too long to make a visit, and by then, my "sting friend Ivy" could have found a stable home in my derriere and sprouted off a little offspring.

Now I know the left hand comes in handy in different cultures, and I have subconsciously noted that a right-hand shake has to be the go in the future. But given that we have been advised it should be "no shake" at the moment, I don't think this is going to be a problem.

This leaves us working on the shoulder greeting bump or maybe fist knock and even the new bum bump. Well, maybe not. Everything may not be in pristine, tip-top condition just at this very moment.

Now at last I understand that I have it all wrong. Toilet paper is just for the dry off, and we can use a towel for that if necessary. It's time for the new bathroom fixture, time to delve into the savings account, and time for a little fountain of water to tickle the nethers. It's time to clear out the flambé, the chardonnay, the buffet, and the fillet. It's time for the reveal of the spanking-brand-new, toilet-paper-free bidet.

In case you run out of toilet paper, here are
a few extra pages in an emergency.

To be used in dire need.

Last chance….

Don't panic, here is one more page….
following chapters not for use.

JUST A THOUGHT

"I don't want to be stinky poo-poo girl. I want to be a happy flower child."

– Drew Barrymore

SENIOR SAGE

We will not run out of toilet paper. Manufacturers will always ramp up production. And isn't that what friends are for? Instead of bringing a "leek roll" to our next "bring a plate," they can bring a "leak roll." Just for now, this may become more handy.

OK Boomer

SENIORS, IT IS BACK TO THE CLASSROOM.

We have a new language to learn if we are to be relevant and feel relevant moving forward. I know it can be rather confusing, but there is jargon out there we now need to learn.

Our self-esteem wants to know when we are *on fleek* and *dank*, and we don't want to *freek*, not *fleek*, when our grandchildren are *dead*.

See, I told ya, it's not as straightforward as you think. No wonder we oldies are dinosaurs and not *goat*. Yes, we are *goat*—see, now, it really confuses you.

So here goes:

Oldies: *Goat*—An animal, related to the sheep but a lighter build.

Youngies: *Goat*—The greatest of all time.

Oldies: *Dank*—When you haven't opened the basement windows for a while and things are humid, moist and yuck.

Youngies: *Dank*—Something excellent, really cool. Maybe smoked through a pipe sometimes.

Oldies: *Dead*—Gone and buried and over and into eternity.

Youngies: *Dead*—Jumping-for-joy happy.

Oldies: *Thirsty*—When you have taken a very long walk in very hot sun with very abundant sweat and now your parched tongue screams out for liquid to hydrate your way home.

Youngies: *Thirsty*—Horny. Not advisable to get this one mixed up. "Excuse me, I am very *thirsty*. Can you help me to rehydrate?"

Oldies: *Woke*—The past tense of *wake*—wakey, wakey, time to rise.

Youngies: *Woke*—To become aware.

Oh, that's right, we have woken up to stuff that is going on in our world at the moment.

Oldies: *Spilling the tea*—Not a good thing to do for burn avoidance.

Youngies: *Spilling the tea*—It's all about sharing the gossip.

Oldies: *Hot tea*—Be even more careful in drinking this hot beverage for burn avoidance.

Youngies: *Hot tea*—It's *hot* gossip; it's GMT.

Oldies: *GMT*—Greenwich Mean Time. Everyone knows that.

Youngies: *GMT*—No, no, no, getting me tight and upset. Yeah, the Greenwich has just got mean.

Oldies: *Salty*—Chips and tinned soup and smoked salmon. All salty and bad for blood pressure.

Youngies: *Salty*—Getting upset over something little.

How did this ever manifest?
Well, seniors, just keep on learning.

Oldies: *Troll*—The little creatures with long coloured hair that we used to brush and tie and brush and tie.

Youngies: *Troll*—Yes, that someone (usually anonymous) who upsets someone on the internet.

Oldies: *Bounce*—Problem that arises when you want to go braless.

Youngies: *Bounce*—When you have to leave a place quickly. Okay, it's the shortened form of *bouncer* that we knew all about in our clubbing days. Got it!

Oldies: *Gucci*—Yes, we like this one. We spend many years saving up for one of these.

Youngies: *Gucci*—Good, doing well, feeling fine. Yes, we do feel fine also when we buy a Gucci

Oldies: *Ship*—Where we all love to travel but can't at this present moment. It may have changed, however, by the time you read this book.

Youngies: *Ship*—When you want two people to become an item.

Really, how does a large watercraft fit into a relationship? Oh, maybe it's just about sailing off into the partner horizon, bingeing on an overabundance of food and wine. Maybe there is a connection.

Oldies: *Jomo*—Only Jomo I know is Jomo Kenyatta, first president of Kenya

Youngies: *Jomo*—Joy of missing out.

Maybe that is what happened under Jomo's rule. I am sure there were many who experienced the joy of missing out.

Oldies: *Fire*—Hot as hell, and scary as hell when it gets out of control.
Youngies: *Fire*—Something is cool.

You see, we think diametrically opposite on some things. But need to understand this divide.

Oldies: *Chewing the fat*—Chitter-chatter and small talk
Youngies: *Chewing the fat*—Never heard of it, sounds disgusting, even on paleo.
Oldies: *Rattling on*—Talking about inane stuff for far too long.
Youngies: *Rattling on*—What we do when we leave and our bones rattle on home.
Oldies: *Cut the gas*—Be quiet
Youngies: *Cut the gas*—Stop farting; we know your muscles are weaker, but you can at least try to hold it in.
Oldies: *Don't sell me a dog*—Don't lie to me.
Youngies: *Don't sell me a dog*—That's right, don't sell me a dog. I have nowhere to put it.

It is all a little confusing, but we are up for learning. Just be patient with us, it's like learning French.

My darling children, Dad and I are *goat*, so *cut the gas.* We have become *fire* and feel *Gucci* about it all. We don't get *salty* about much, so don't you get GMT. We are now going to *bounce* for some *hot tea.* We are on *fleek. Don't clap back* (a comeback filled with attitude)

You say, "OK, BOOMER."

We say, "BYE, FELICIA," (an expression used to dismiss someone).

See, we are fast learners!

JUST A THOUGHT

"It's better being a Felicia than a Karen," I say.

SENIOR SAGE

Time to cross the generational divide, don't ya think?

I Swallowed a Watermelon Pip

SOMETIMES MY BRAIN IS FULL OF WHACKY THOUGHTS.

They generally attack just prior to slumber but can sometimes surface on my long Saturday walk when my brain is unlocked for exploration. Maybe my brain has been playing companion to my body while locked in and is bursting with the joy of release into wide-open and thought-provoking spaces.

I am not becoming alternate, just exploring the abstract and unusual. It is simply called creativity, and it is a wonderful awakening, is it not?

My academic friends may call it something else—maybe "kooky" would fit the bill?

Yes, I am aware that this is not academia, but academia can become a little dull sometimes, can it not? So here is a little left field to sparkle up the day.

I swallowed a watermelon pip, and I think that is exactly why my girth is expanding. It is merrily growing an offspring that is preparing to win the blue ribbon at the next Agricultural show.

Is the girth maybe expanding as I dug a bit too deep into watermelon heaven today, or has so-called pip found a place in my gut to embed and proliferate?

I scamper to my online lecturer.

No, this abdominal spread has absolutely nothing to do with the pip ingestion but rather more so the pack of gingernuts—gluten-free, of course—I discovered in the pantry. I had forgotten they were there, as co-senior had sneakily found a hiding place for fear of a drop in self-esteem after my daily morning scale session.

So, I find out that watermelon pips are actually quite good for you; it's the cherries and the apples that are not quite so.

Of course, they are packed with oodles of goodness, but the pip—nah, nah.

Too many of these contain "cyanide" I understand. *Cyanide*—I thought that chemical only showed its face in spy movies to wipe out the unsuspecting victim.

So maybe my thoughts weren't so radical. Some pips do and some pips don't, and I needed to have the knowledge to work out which one was which.

Did you know that the best part of a cucumber tastes like the worst part of a watermelon? Useless information I know, but just a bit of fun.

This thought bubble is now laid to rest.

So, what do people see when they walk behind me? I can't see me behind me. I can never see my face—only the reflection of my face in a mirror or on my phone.

Do people's organs feel like my organs?

Do their livers and kidneys and arms feel like mine? I can't feel what they feel.

What are my eyeballs looking at when my eyes are shut? My inner eyelids?

And to top it all.....

Numbers have a start, but they never have an end.

I stare out of the window, glad to take a rest from my unusual thoughts.

But then it starts raining, and all I can think of is that everything is having a good wash, and that means everything, good and bad (as in *virus* bad) could go down the drain.

So, should we start touching again, or if we are compelled to still wear masks, should we throw in a few M&Ms so we can snack attack like an Argentinian stallion between chuckers?

Why is lipstick called *lipstick* if we can still move our lips? Who cares? Nobody sees our lips these days. Thank goodness, as the mask is producing some nasty little critters outside the lipliner parameters. And on that, who cares about Botox around the mouth? I need full use of all my mouth muscles And what if…?

Stop, Julie, go to sleep—there is too much weirdness going on here. But then again, I am an original, and a little bit of quirk here and there never hurts. It could quirkily send me off to sleep.

JUST A THOUGHT

"Is it weird in here, or is it just me?"

– Steven Wright

SENIOR SAGE

We are all a little weird to someone else in some way or another. This is what makes us human.

Virtual Travel

I HEAR A PLANE OVERHEAD. IT IS THE FIRST TIME IN A long time. The flight path over our house has been silent for so very long.

The roar of the engines is enticing and addictive, and oh how I wish I were also floating between the clouds.

I will never grumble again about cramped spaces. I have become an expert on cramped spaces this year. I will embrace airline food and turbulence and smelly feet.

I will passionately absorb it all as I want to see you again—Italy, France, Spain, USA, UK, Middle East, Israel, Croatia, friends, my children, my grandchildren, the world.

My feet are itchy. We have lost a year.

I want to taste your food again. I want to absorb your culture again. I want to hear your mother tongue again. I want to feel again.

I will never be complacent. My heart will explode in gratitude.

I will set foot on your soil again.

This is our time for travel now, is it not, seniors? (For those who love to travel, that is.) The brochures with travel aspirations are slowly coming back into print.

And we begin to dream once again.

So let's imagine. Let's dream. Let's create our travel vision board for the future.

Settle in, dear seniors. I promise, it will be a smooth ride.

ITALY

You are sitting in the Basilica of Santa Maria, one of the oldest churches in Trastevere, Rome.

You are still and feel this mighty dynasty surrounding your soul. You hear the church bells of a neighbouring church.

"*Bellisimo, bellisimo*!" as a new bride glides down the aisle.

"*Bravo, bravo*," from the patrons at the taverna with chequered tablecloths, located right opposite.

You taste the perfection of pizza and oozing mozzarella.

You smell the aroma of freshly baked pastries.

You stand amongst locals and ignite your day with a dark morning expresso.

You are immersed in the layered conversations of *si*, *per favore*, *grazie*, *prego*, *mi scusi*, *mi dispiace*, and *buon giorno* as you stand in front of an artistic masterpiece of Florence.

Your brain consumes the image of Michelangelos's *David* and Botticelli's *Birth of Venus*. You walk down uneven cobbled streets in search of Renaissance riches.

You climb the steps of the Duomo.

You breathe in the deep, luscious smell of leather displayed by the market vendors.

Imagine. Just imagine. Are you there?

You breathe in the salty air of the Amalfi Coast.

You feel the water lapping around your ankles, embracing your toes. You sip on Vino Rosso. You sing "O Sole Mio."

Take a sip of your coffee, and breathe in deeply.

MIDDLE EAST

You watch the dawn rising in the pallet of your mind and hear the morning prayers echo from the horizon.

The taste of honey baklava sweetens the tip of your tongue.

You breathe in oriental spices floating through the atmosphere.

You feel the spray of sand under camel's feet and the whisper of the wind floating through an organza tent surrounding a succulent feast.

You slowly amble down well-worn cobbled streets through the Holy City, absorbing history and the incense of spirituality and vapours of conflicting but homogeneous religions.

Are you there? Can you feel it? Can you smell it? Can you touch it?

AFRICA

You breathe in the breath of Africa and the musky aroma of wild grass and wild animals.

Your heart beats to the rhythm of the drum. You are mesmerised by tribal chants and ululations.

You hear the power of the king of the jungle as he commands his authority in resounding roars.

Transport yourself, dear seniors, and be present deep down in the depths of your subconscious. What a thrilling day it will be.

HAWAII

Find a ukulele in your imaginary mind travel.

Sway your hips to the beat, and hear the rustles of your grass skirt as the strands skim each other in playful harmony. You shout out "*Aloha*," recognising the deep, sweet smell of pineapple.

You are lost in a kaleidoscope of colour and the deep azure of the sea and breathe in holiday and sunsets and new friendships.

You feel the warmth of the setting sun on your skin.

It's all there, right there, dear seniors. You have a world to discover. It is only as far away as your imagination.

This is only the start.

We will visit these places again.

Keep on saving.

The best is yet to come.

JUST A THOUGHT

"The real voyage of discovery consists not in seeking new landscapes, but in having new eyes."

– *Marcel Proust*

SENIOR SAGE

Some people may love to travel, and some may not. But I know from my experiences that from every journey travelled, something always remains and is stored safely in the memory bank to withdraw at any time. At this later stage in life, and in this unusual predicament we are in, this album of memories and adventures is so joyous to once again unfold while our brains take a little rest from the noise and commotion that usually surrounds us in life.

After You

IT TOOK FOREVER TO EXIT THE LIFT TODAY. EVERYBODY was being ever so gracious and polite.

"After you."

"No, after you."

"After you."

This unique behaviour seems to have been developed from our lengthy isolation.

We are all so incredibly happy to be in the company of other people and to communicate with someone—anyone! Now, at last we have human contact again. Well, not actually contact; contact, but arm's-length contact. We have banded together as the glorious harmonious tribe of the "After yous."

Ok, so let's go back a few steps.

I have a question. Is there a pecking order in lift etiquette?

Are the "oldies" ushered out first as a sign that respect is still well and blossoming, or are oldies left to bring up the rear as they shuffle and are slow and irritating?

Co-senior says, "After you," to the mother with screaming twins seated in her trolley. I know he is portraying so much loveliness, but the truth of the matter is that his graciousness is a by-product of muddled hearing. His interpretation of a baby's scream is bomb-alert piercing. It is deafening and confusing, and he wants them out. He wants them out *tout de suite.*

Mother with twins says, "After you," to co-senior as she thinks he looks a bit dodgy and she doesn't want him to collapse into her trolley on top of her beloveds.

A frazzled shopper at the back of the lift says, "After you," to the teenager in front who has sneezed all over the dials that she had to press to get to the next floor. She is now in defence mode as her mask has disappeared amongst the bananas. Her hand sanitiser is lost amongst the conglomeration in her bag that hasn't been sorted or discarded for months whilst in hibernation. There are so many discarded, used masks making friends in her bag that a hand dip could stir up some very nasty germy air.

With her inner elbow now firmly attached to her lips and her outer elbow ready for the button push, she appears ready to capture a new TikTok moment.

I am last in line and don't say, "After You," to anyone, as my claustrophobia and germaphobia are playing tag, and I want to get out of there as fast as my social distancing will allow.

So, as you can see,we are locked in a pod of confusion as the lift closes amidst our "After yous," and we are imprisoned for another few floors while the lift automation shows its confusion as well.

Worse still, there is a distinct smell of rotten eggs in the lift, not coming from my basket but from someone who has gorged some unhealthy feast the night before. The innocent start to frown, and the perpetrator turns up the verbal volume with a distinct indication of "guilty." Thank goodness social distancing is aerating the situation. This, mixed with the flowery perfume exuding from mumma of twins, who is trying to disguise the spew on her T-shirt, is a veritable mess and reminds me that I would never ever want to be an aromachologist.

And then there is light, the elevator door slides open, and freedom beckons. All degrees of gallantry have dissolved and with arms outstretched and abdomens tightened we all rush out like galloping crosses, still adhering to the rules of no touch, no cough.

Oh well, it's fourteen days since that encounter and everything still appears to be normal. Except—I forgot to tell you—my thigh muscles are now looking very taut and terrific as they have graduated to the shopping centre stair climb. The stairs don't seem to be everyone's first option. We are a lazy bunch in our suburb. I spread my wings, just because. There is no one in sight. I am social distancing by choice, and as I breathe in deep, I release all contagious "After you" tension.

JUST A THOUGHT

"Life is like an elevator, a lot of ups and downs. People pushing your buttons and getting jerked around."

– Lecrae

SENIOR SAGE

Walk up the stairs and the ramps. The muscles you develop will serve you well as you age. Nothing pouffs up after the age of seventy-three, so they say. So get going, seniors, and start moving. Who wants to get an elevated temperature from the elevator ride?

The Driveway Dash

WRITTEN WHILE STILL IN SEMI-LOCKDOWN.

We all know that things are currently unusual.

From what we understand, if most of us settle into domesticity for a period, we can knock this invading contagion into oblivion, and we can all step into our spring dresses with spring in our steps, glorifying the fact that we have survived it all and eternally grateful that we and our senior friends are all safe and healthy in a different world on the other side.

The situation is seriously working on our cognitive state (which is a good thing) as we endeavour to remember what we can touch and with what. We are continually educated by medical experts on what must come off and what has to stay on, and when and how and should we, could we, must we, and every other question lurking in our fearful subconscious.

No wonder we are fearful.

From what we can see, the world is now closed for business. No more senior moments in cafes and bars (that is infrequent anyway). No more golf outings or swimming or even the beaches and, calamity, the remedial massage for the achy knees and shoulders. No, we are now limited to emergencies—grocery shopping, doctors, and pills (lots of those) with an added addition to the pillbox to curb this new anxiety ailment.

But there is one tiny ray of light called "the hairdresser". Despite the fact that we need to be our own height away from each other and are covered by lifesaving preventative gear, it's fine for our friendly hairdresser to stand just a face and a half away to ensure we are hearing the latest gossip circulating in the salon, mostly, at present about viral contamination.

We feel unsettled, however, as we don't know if our hairdresser has been settling in with non-symptom virus-bearing friends and is unremittingly spreading viral content amongst our freshly coloured locks.

Well, in all honesty, hair *can be* an emergency, so I can see how this was locked in with lifesaving paramedics and respiratory surgeons. (Tongue-in-cheek, of course.)

Leaving the salon with a Pro Hart boldly splashed across my facemask, after a sneaky colour touch-up, I open the car door gingerly and proceed to ensure that I follow step one to step ten in how to disinfect and de-robe before arriving back at the front door.

There is a problem.

I have touched the car door handle with the same gloves that touched the counter in the salon where the hairdryer has been placed, which has blown another suspect's hair who has had an unauthorised coffee with an international friend who has just flown in from a country where currently there is a boom in coffin manufacturers and whose second cousin has recently surrendered to an infection. Whew, that was a long explanation.

Chestnut-brown conditioning colour was maybe not worth it this time. Little grey ladies with red lipstick can still look very fashionable.

So, with sidewards glances from passing drivers at my anime eyes peering through misty glasses, with a face covered by an industrial "Hannibal Lecter" type mask (no wonder the hairdresser wanted me out fast—actually, I think she wanted to go home herself), I drive home at pace. I can't quite work out whether drivers are trying to decipher the back end of the human apparition in the car in front of them or are darn annoyed with themselves for waiting too late to buy my fashion accessory.

I breathe a sigh of relief as I drive up to my front door. I have arrived home alive despite the fact that there is a distinct lack of oxygen around my claustrophobic mouth.

What went on now must come off.

With hands in the air mimicking an imminent surgical procedure to be performed by myself, of course, I deftly open the car door with my elbow. Flinging myself out of the door, hands in air, I at last locate my pink antiseptic with blue sparkle gel, which I have misplaced in the journey home. The gel has happily been cocooned in the intergluteal cleft and now on release squirts its innards in its entirety into my newly bought bag, which doesn't, by the way, need disinfecting.

The family are standing at the front door performing their traffic attendant skills as I now have to de-robe without any anti-contagion accessories and, at the risk of complete family banishment, can't touch my face.

With inventive entrepreneurship I break off a branch from my favourite lemon tree, hook this under surgical gloves, and flick off with aplomb. I can now release my contusioned face from face isolation, and with confidence completely undress right there in the driveway.

With the assurance of a long-standing member of a nudist society, I saunter into the kitchen to reach the finish line—the twenty second (as long as it takes to sing "Happy Birthday") anti-virus, between the fingers and up the arm, hand wash.

The family freeze in stationary bewilderment.

I hear the neighbour's lawnmower no more. They have become voyeurs, staring, collapsed at the vision of unbridled swaying body parts striding towards our front door. They may think we are very strange, and there may be a fallout. We will work on the relationship when the world settles down. But thank goodness, I am home, and I remain safe.

JUST A THOUGHT

"We all came naked, and we shall all depart naked."

– Aesop, 620–560 BC, ancient Greek fabulist

SENIOR SAGE

Keep antibacterial/viral handwash everywhere—in your bag, in your pocket, on the kitchen bench, in the car. It could save your life.

Everyone Has a Trigger

"WHAT'S TO EAT?" I CALL OUT TO CO-SENIOR AS I lounge in front of the TV screen.

"What's to eat?" repeats co-senior. "Haven't we just had dinner?"

"Yes, but I still feel like a snackerel."

"OK, what would you like?" he responds as he slowly slides off the couch to search the pantry.

"Anything nice that you can find!"

So nice? Why is "nice" holding hands with too much sugar, too much fat, and too much salt?

The nibble marathon begins, and I can't find the finish line. The disappointment in lack of willpower will be tangible tomorrow. We have given it a rest today.

So why do it?

What has created the "Marathon Snack Monster?"

What is the trigger?

Some will say it is time for therapy, some will say it is time for deep reflection, and some will say, "Shut your mouth; it is only a bad habit." "Be disciplined," they insist.

I have tried the "be disciplined" and shut-your-mouth approach. It is not working. An abstract thread seems to be opening and shutting my mouth, and I can't find the origin.

What has upset me today that I seek the solace of "something nice"? What has upset you today that you do the same?

There is a trigger, so be still, be calm, breathe and identify it.

♥

I was in a room in a unit in South Africa. It was a good time. Our family, my parents, my sister, and I were on holiday.

Part of our holiday relaxation agenda was to go to movies. We love movies. We relax in movies. We are though, at the mercy of the local cinema's offering. Sometimes this isn't a perfect match for a little underage girl.

We do try once to slip in unnoticed to a gory war story, but when the blood and guts and trauma jump out of the screen into our vivid imaginations, we depart rapidly knowing that age restrictions are there for a reason and my parents hope that there isn't any long-term trauma from the visual horror.

This doesn't stop the family outings at the cinema.

Next time it would be different. It most certainly was.

There was no next time for me.

The family primped and primed for a night out, while I watched from the shadows of my makeshift sleeping area. They were excited for their night out. I was apprehensive. The unit was secure, and I was sensible and engrossed in my new book. Someone they happened to know would check in to see if I was OK. They wouldn't be long. They departed, and I was so afraid.

The noises floating in from outside seemed dark and angry and unknown. The shadows on the walls seemed more black and ominous. The words in my book seemed more challenging and sinister. We had no mobile or landline. There was no form of contact.

I watched the dial on the unfamiliar wooden clock.

Tick-tock. Tick-tock....watching the minutes and the seconds circle and circle.

I am left out, and I don't like it.

♥

I have beautiful friends. Some of these friends go way, way back.

My friends are diverse and interesting and loyal. They don't fit into groups, nor do I wish them to. I am not a "groupie".

Everyone appears to jostle for leadership in a group. There seems to be an obvious survival-instinct agenda with an undercurrent of social politicking. Everyone jousts for leadership supremacy. Some thrive in this environment, while others wilt. It is exhausting.

I invite my two BFFs to dinner with their current partners. They vaguely know each other.

The dinner is an immense success. My besties became besties themselves, locked in meaningful conversations. I become the host/waiter feeding them titbits to enhance their connection.

That night I am invisible.

They are singing in harmony, completely in tune.

Countless dinners and occasions and coffees ensue without me. I am not invited.

I am left out, and I don't like it.

And now we are adults, and we are more carefree and dismissive of this. It's not that we have been left out; we have simply moved on. That season was then, and this season is now. We have grown up.

We shouldn't worry if our comment is the only one that hasn't been liked on our Facebook pages.

We shouldn't worry if the family has a group email and we are not included.

We shouldn't worry if all receive a gift while we don't.

We shouldn't worry if a lunch date doesn't include us.

But sometimes, we still do.

We want so badly to trust in loyalty, enabling us to lower our walls of protection.

Surely our life experience has made us our own people.

If an occasion doesn't warrant our inclusion, it is not a betrayal—there is something better out there for us.

We are not rejected but *re-directed*, and that is awesome in its discovery.

♥

As co-senior rustles in the pantry to find a comforting snack, I try to work out who left me out today. If I don't remember right now, that is still fine as at last I have identified my trigger and the handful of blueberries I ate after dinner will absolutely and completely suffice.

JUST A THOUGHT

"One remedy for the fear of not being loved is to remember how good it feels to love someone. If you're feeling unloved and you want to feel better, go love someone, and see what happens."

– *Dossie Easton*

SENIOR SAGE

Recognise that when the nibbling starts and won't stop, it's time to take a breath and work out why. It could be all that is needed is a good night's sleep or a bottle of hydrating water.

When It's Time to Evacuate

AUSTRALIA IS ON FIRE.

The news bulletin bombards us with images of singed koalas and burning kangaroos surrounded by a background of red and flaming-orange burning infernos.

The land is dry, and we are paying the price. Our beautiful verdant forests are now barren, crumbling sticks. These sparse remnants expel their burning ash-like confetti through the air, invading our eyes, our throats and our lives, and we are sad.

Our hearts are so sore at the loss of our beautiful wildlife and the destitute homeless who have watched their hearth and homes reduce to cinder and their environment engulfed in acrid gloom.

I have experienced fire before. I have slammed hessian bags into flames to stop the spread.

I have watched my family fighting fires on rooftops, fighting with desperation to maintain the status quo.

And here we are again in unprecedented circumstances, some say due to our lack of awareness that our climate is in trouble, and we now pay the price.

I have downloaded an app that continuously updates me on the conditions near my home. Today there are many fires in the "close to home" radius, and we don't sleep well.

I wake up for a bathroom visit in the middle of the night and open the window to see the stars veiled in darkness. The earth smells different.

I freeze.

"Babe," I call, "come quickly," standing in my pyjamas and peering out the window.

"Look."

Co-senior runs to the window, sensing my urgency.

"Look!"

Co-senior peers through the bathroom window at a shimmering orange ball of light at the end of the street, matched with the smell of burning bricks and mortar.

We run downstairs and outside and climb onto the garden wall, straining to see if we are in danger and it is time to go. The light is flickering, and the smoke is thicker.

"Where are our passports?" I frantically call to co-senior.

We stand there for what seems like an eternity.

The flame is not getting bigger. In fact, it remains the same shape, and then—poof!—it is gone. Our neighbour has installed a bright orange light and has now gone to beddy-byes. And we breathe again.

However, danger is creeping closer daily.

Ping—a warning on our electronic device.

A fire is located at the end of our street. It is the only way out of our cul-de-sac. Now things are getting serious.

We wonder whether it would be appropriate to cautiously look before running. Our community Facebook group is in meltdown—some furious that onlookers are blocking the exit pathway, and some scared that their home could be next.

We decide to grab our suitcases from their dusty resting places and run up the stairs to gather our most importants—our passports, medications, computer and charger, spare glasses, a favourite jacket, the last letter from Mum and a piece of one of her dresses immortalising a memory of a happy time together. My guitar and favourite music has a look-in. I grab our code book, share and insurance certificates, banking information, the in-basket, all backup USBs, irreplaceable photos in photo frames and our Bible.

With a grab of some snacks, that is it. We are out of there.

This is all in the middle of the night, and we are planning a little shut-eye in the back of the car if it is not safe to return home.

We can't get near the smoky expanding glow, so we drive around our local area for a while, fully aware that this will either become an impending disaster or we could possibly be back tucked up in bed once our hero "firies" have the flames under control.

We are lucky this night. The glow disperses and the smoke pervades, but we are back under the blankets in a few hours.

We drag the suitcases back into the house the following morning, and LIGHTBULB!!

What would we need exactly if that were all we had left?

If our family and pets are all safe and we have our "we would really cry if we lost it" possessions, then what else? It would be heartbreaking to lose our familiar abode. It would be inconvenient and horrifying and terribly sad. But we can rise from the ashes, just like a phoenix, can we not?

I make a few notes to myself should it happen again.

Some pre-planning may come in useful for you if you end up in the same situation:

- Copy all necessary files onto a USB for quick removal.
- Make sure you are insured and you know where your insurance documents are.
- Make a list of what you would grab if you had to leave in a hurry, and keep this list in a safe place.
- Put all your legal documents and passports in one place for easy access.
- Write down your favourite outfit or coat or article of clothing that you would sorely miss.
- Make a list of any irreplaceable memories or items, meaningful ancestry documents or parchments.
- Back up all photos that cannot be replaced.

When you are in a spin and in this heightened stressful situation, thinking can become scattered.

Follow a list if you are feeling numb, and you will come through on the other side.

If your life is in danger, leave it all behind and run.

We all need so little. It is so liberating when we really, really comprehend this.

JUST A THOUGHT

"Ask yourself, what step can you take today to make your life lighter? What can you let go of that is no longer serving you?"

– *Tova Payne*

SENIOR SAGE

Minimalism is so liberating. We drown in stuff, mostly that we haven't even looked at for an awfully long time. We are lost in the mess. Clear it out, and your mind will do the same. And you will be free.

Craft

THERE IS AN INTERMINABLE WAIT AT THE POST OFFICE today. This is compounded by the fact that we all have to queue one and a half metres apart.

The line is out the door and around the coffee shop. I almost abort for a cappuccino but decide against it as the postage of parcels is now an urgent mission that must be accomplished. There is a birthday on the other side of the world, and we need to be present on the day.

The line is moving very slowly, partly due to participants being lured into stopping at all the shelves on the way for some unneeded and unwanted item. The line is becoming the new meet-and-greet to find new friends. The atmosphere is congenial in frustration. I decide to breathe and go for the ride.

I am nearly there.

There is only one person before me.

She is dressed in her best, she carries a walking stick, her glasses are perched, her grey hair is coiffed. She is as sharp as a tack.

She fumbles in her bag while balancing her stick. I move forward to assist, endeavouring to not compromise personal space.

She is mumbling. I think she is mumbling at me.

I hear her repeating the word "CRAFT". I assume she has picked up the pom-pom maker on the final stand as a new craft for a grandchild.

"Can I help you?" I enquire.

"I always need help," she says. "Do you know I am ninety?"

"Ninety!" I exclaim. "Oh, my goodness, I would never have thought so."

"I feel ninety sometimes," I add.

"You are awesome," I continue, "*and* I see that you are looking for craft for some lucky girl or boy. I see there is a whole craft section right here. Can I help you choose something?"

She stands tall and looks me straight in the eye.

"I'm not looking for craft, dear. I am trying to find my account to pay, but I think I have left it at home!"

"Ninety can sometimes be rather challenging," she continues.

"I ***C.****an't* ***R.****emember* ***A. F.****ucking* ***T****hing.*"

She said it, not me. Roll on ninety, I think there are going to be some fun times ahead!

JUST A THOUGHT

I cannot see
I cannot pee,
I cannot chew,
I cannot screw,
Oh my god, what can I do?
My memory shrinks,
My hearing stinks,
No sense of smell,
I look like hell,
My mood is bad - can you tell?
My body's drooping,
Have trouble pooping,
The Golden Years,
Have come at last;
The Golden Years can kick my ass.

– From "The Cat in the Hat on Aging"

SENIOR SAGE

Oh, how glorious that age brings freedom of expression. No fear, no judgement, just is as it is. Perfection in its imperfection.

Love Greatly While You Still Can

THE FACE OF A BEAUTIFUL OLDER WOMAN IN BELGIUM jumped out from our newsfeed today. This angel is now departed, well over on the other side.

In her dying moment, she refused the lifesaving ventilator, telling doctors to save it for younger patients. She said she had lived a full and happy life and would rather gift the same to the much younger patient lying beside her.

These stricken victims of our unexpected Third World War (just of a different kind) are leaving this universe, attached to emergency resuscitation equipment, of course, if they are lucky, or in passages of overwrought hospitals where the tyranny of extreme numbers has overrun the ability for an insufficient stressed health system to assist. Doesn't the notion of this abject aloneness in death make your heart bleed?

If you are a senior reading this book, you are older now, and as each day passes, we all cleave closer to those who make us feel safe and loved. We don't really need much more than that. In our creation, maybe our ancestors and we and our offspring and their offspring are all just one, and we are each selected in each generation, out of this mass, to be implanted singularly on this earth that we know. Maybe our genetics and mass and souls are one large cell of osmosis.

So now, when the circle of life reaches its last triangle, moving slowly to the end (like watching an app download if you are of the "now" generation) these beautiful human souls, forced by a virus that no one yet understands, float back into eternity, leaving their genetic cell lineage without a farewell.

They lie in isolation, imprisoned by masks and lifesaving oxygen, fighting for the chance once again to hold their loved ones and say, "I love you. I really do."

Strange medical representatives hold their hands, if they get there in time, and assure them that all will be OK. But it isn't OK, and a treasured family member is no more.

Doesn't it make you feel sad and rather helpless, just like they felt?

Family members wait in sorrow, in their own isolation, and scream in their inadequacy and their powerlessness. How desperate are they to hold and love and share and combine just one more time?

One minute a family in its completeness is bantering around a dining table, and "nanna and pappa" are rebutting jokes that are made, playfully, at their expense. Connection and love and mirth and spirit combines. The next they are lying in anguished solitude with no genetic comfort surrounding them and strangers looking through their eyes when they utter their final words.

This situation will eventually simmer down and end. We will find prophylactic concoctions to prevent the spread, and life will continue, even though in a new kind of world.

Children will be at the bedside of their older loved ones. Good-byes will be real and loving and shared and gentle and so very sad. Connection will be there right in the room, holding on to the physical until the spiritual flies away.

Nobody expected or even imagined that this viral situation could occur. We watch "Contagion" movies with storylines that we now seem to be duplicating. We scoff between each other that nothing so pervasively frightening could ever happen. We are in scientific nirvana. The minds of scientists are so sophisticated, they can map the human genome. They understand gene editing, but now they are in a desperate battle with time to work out how to halt this deathly spread.

The loss of your loved "older one" could be sudden and unexpected. It could be a broken hip or a hidden cancer or a motor vehicle error. Life can end suddenly, unexpectedly or alone. So, shower the people you love with love, my beautiful peeps. Always answer the phone when a loved one calls. You don't want any regrets. You never want to be too late.

JUST A THOUGHT

"No one is useless in this world who lightens the burdens of another."

– Charles Dickens

SENIOR SAGE

You never know what the next year, month, hour, minute or second will bring. Things can change in a minute. Call your family, friends and loved ones. The voicemail message may be the only time you will ever hear their voice again.

Gender Bender

IT IS CHRISTMAS CELEBRATION TIME, LONG BEFORE the limited celebrations of 2020.

Company party invitations are prodigious in their volume. Some look like so much fun, a welcome reward after a year of hard work and escalating profits.

Co-senior's company party is themed and sounds like fun.

The French Revolution—not so fun.

As this party is close to home, it is time to dig out our best dress-up innovations. Secretly we wonder if an inventive resourceful costume could even assist in a promotion. It is time to put in a little effort and use our lateral thinking skills. We need a good disguise. We need to stand out and be noticed.

I loathe dress-up parties and the hypocritical gaiety that goes with it.

"Ooh, you look so good."

"Wow, who are you?"

Maybe this is post-traumatic stress from my early days when I arrived at a "Spaced Out" party dressed as a

"Mars-mellow" and inappropriately and awkwardly blended in amongst a haze of piney, skunky grass.

At these dress-ups, there is always a single melancholy hermit wearing a themed hat as an accessory to show they have given it a go. They really, really don't want to be there. Judgement of effort is always profound, and we all screech in false mirth and backslap with vigour while silently trying to decipher how to de-robe to have at least a crack at the "ladies' room" without embarrassing accident.

This goes on for hours—or should I say until the first couple of cocktails have kicked in, after which we really don't give a hoot.

It is all consuming!

For this work occasion, the visit to the hire costume company proves successful. We leave as a French lieutenant and a buxom wench, and we are now fully prepared.

The children are certainly unprepared as co-senior decides to give the outfits a trial run and comes flying round the corner, just prior to children's shut-eye, fully robed, as a very buxom French wench (Mrs. Doubtfire-like) mop cap and wig awry. The kids shriek in delight.

It is now unanimous. Roles are going to be reversed, and my offering for the evening is now French lieutenant.

It works out quite well actually, as I caught a streaming cold on the morning of the celebration and didn't really want to do much talking. I was quite happy behind the "kepi" and trousers with a bunch of pockets where copious tissues and menthol were happily nestled, waiting to jump to the rescue.

We order a cab. The cabbie driver is bemused and bewildered. But hey, we live in modern times, so maybe cross dressing is prevalent in the 'burbs.

Co-senior booms out the direction to a friend's house along the way. It is his moment to preen in French lace and froufrou, and he is rather enjoying his one-day transformation.

The front door to our friend's house is unlocked.

Two of their early teen boys are huddled in the lounge room, deeply engrossed in Nintendo. They have foregone television entertainment tonight as the last offering of *Silence of the Lambs* had left them unnerved, and the *Legend of Zelda* was abundantly more relaxing, while parents were dining with their friends in the next room.

Co-senior flings open the door, races into the house, all six foot of him, in a flourish of petticoats and lace.

The boys freeze.

The friends hit the floor and crawl under the table to avoid injury in this home invasion.

And, with not a word spoken, co-senior flies back out the front door and, with a ripple of pouf, dives back into the car.

"Drive," he belts out to the cabbie.

Co-senior wins first prize at the company party for best-dressed female.

My cold gets better.

The preteen boys have nightmares.

Our friends are still our friends......AND

Co-senior is promoted.

JUST A THOUGHT

"This transition has been harder on me than anything I could imagine. And that's the case for so many others besides me. For that reason alone, trans people deserve something vital. They deserve your respect. And from that respect comes a more compassionate community, a more empathetic society, and a better world for all of us."

– Caitlyn Jenner

SENIOR SAGE

Oh, how beautiful to be whatever you want to be and not care about what others think. It is the ultimate freedom.

Online Is Our Master

I AM ON STANDBY THIS MORNING AND VERY ALERT.

My fingers have become extraordinarily nimble recently, scrolling through online shopping sites. I really don't need anything, but it has become rather addictive. I also forget that the models that are draped in new fashion trends don't look like me. They are so tall and so slim and look so good, so any new outfit will never ever look same-same.

Today I am ready to leap to attention.

I need to get to the front door before co-senior. I hope the parcel arrives on his gym day.

We are serious about budgeting at the moment, so I know I shouldn't really be sneaky.

"Parcels arrived," co-senior shouts from downstairs.

Oh damn, I think, *co-senior hasn't left for gym.*

"I'll get it," I shout from upstairs.

"Can't hear you!" co-senior shouts from downstairs.

"I'll get it." I turn it up a decibel.

I hear the thud on the floor outside.

"Knock, knock, parcel" our contactless delivery person shouts.

"Thank you," I shout halfway down the stairs.

Co-senior arrives at the front door before me, and we collide at the entrance.

"What's the rush?" asks co-senior.

"Oh, nothing" I reply.

He opens the door and rotates the parcel, looking for its origin.

I grab it from him. "I'll take it upstairs."

"What is it?" he asks.

"Not sure," I say. "I think I took advantage of sale time to get a pressie for our little one. I'll keep it for his birthday."

"Mmm," he mumbles as he hands me a soft, flat, light package.

I take it upstairs, quickly unwrap it, love what I see and hurl it to the rear of the cupboard to expose it again when the finances look rosier.

Co-senior leaves for gym, and I fly back into the cupboard to try on the new outfit. It doesn't fit. The top is too big, and the bottom too small. And now there is the whole lengthy process of finding the initial wrapping in one piece, completing the documentation and packaging up again for return.

Co-senior returns from gym.

Before settling in, I ask him if he could please, please, *pretty please* hop back into the car and drop a parcel into the post office.

He is not happy, but I am the love of his life, so he likes to keep me happy.

"Is this not right for the grandkids?" he enquires, making note that the parcel looks exactly the same as the morning delivery.

"No, wrong size," I offer as a throwaway line.

Well, technically it is the truth. It is the wrong size, so no deceit going on here.

I hear the car move out of the driveway and return to folding the socks with my tail between my legs.

I don't like to tell little white ones. But we are all on top of each other all the time at the moment. There is no extra space for flexibility around the truth edges. Not even a teeny-weensy bit.

I climb the stairs and open the cupboard. My old favourites greet me. They have no new friend to brighten up their space.

I open co-senior's drawer to put away his socks. And there, nestled between the underwear, I feel something unusual. My hand scrambles around and hey presto, six Snickers bars deliciously jump out to greet me.

Aaaah!!! It appears that co-senior has his own little sneaky side hustle going on.

At first this is unsettling, as co-senior tells me everything—or so I think.

But I now know why. The bars have been on special at the local supermarket and have become too hard to resist. I have forcefully advised co-senior that this was the week I was not to be tempted with anything that could affect my COVID-kilo weight-loss plan. Hence the subterfuge. He is forgiven.

I now don't feel so bad and plonk myself down on the bed with one of my finds oozing from my mouth. I am drooling and in heaven. I will fess up to co-senior when he arrives home. We can drown in chocolate deliciousness together.

And who cares about the COVID kilos—tomorrow is another day.

JUST A THOUGHT

It's funny when people try to be sneaky when the only person they are fooling is themselves.

SENIOR SAGE

I am sure we all tell little white lies now and then to exaggerate the narrative. Problem is, if you are not truthful, you will always be found out. You will never remember the fib, but others will, and you will just end up in a meatloaf of pickles.

Suspicious Minds

I HAVE A NEW TAI CHI MOVE. THE TRADITIONAL NAME is "White Crane spreads its wing," but my new manouevre is "White Dame spreads its wing." I have to say it is very unusual but has been borne out of necessity as I am now competing in the category of goody-good, rule-abiding, social-distancing champion.

We have been told that we need to spread the distance of human contact by meterage of at least an outstretched arm, and I am very aware that for my safety I need to abide by instructions.

I fully understand that it may look like I have completely lost it and am about to charge down the supermarket aisle with wings flapping ready for takeoff into the frozen food section. But this T-shaped body form is merely to protect myself from a passerby who feels the whole situation we are all in is merely a conspiracy and who cares if a few of us oldies drop off. It's the will of the universe, they say. It's the Boomer Remover revolution.

We are all encased now in a nucleus of suspicion.

Who has it; who hasn't?

Who is sniffing? Worse, who is coughing?

Who is wearing masks? Why are they not wearing masks?

A glowering scowl is now our new accessory, and our passive-aggressive, sotto voce "I can't believe people can be so selfish" is the line always at front of brain when we pass a non-rule-abiding passerby.

We started out in this "thing" all lovely, chanting "we are all in this together". Now we are irritated at confinement, irritated at lack of free breaths, irritated at adjusting to a new world and very irritated at those who don't care that we are more vulnerable and who feel we deserve to be the first to fall as payback for our entitled lives.

This "suspicia" (not the name of an *Addams Family* parody—and not even a word but feeling right on this occasion) has now moved into suburbia.

At last, we are allowed to have family around to the house—but only a certain number of the family. So, pity poor number five, six and seven family members as their turn in the get-together relay will have to continue next week.

But herein lies more suspicion.

The littlies scream up the driveway as they see their nannas, gaggas, pappas, oupas, gaggle of geriatrics again, and unknowingly fling their arms up in the air for a throw in the air. This cannot be ignored as, quite frankly, what is life all about?

However, on family departure, suspicious thoughts once again come back to visit and terrorise. The littlies had a little sniff, and we kissed them all over, and they are still going to preschool. And what if Harper, who played dolls with them, and Archie, who played Transformers with them have been to a restaurant nearby where a cluster has eventuated? And they, asymptomatically, have now infected us, and we are headed for the ICU.

Suspicion creates more suspicion, and we would probably now be able to open our own investigation unit to follow up on everyone who in our tortured minds is surely guilty.

Well, one good thing that has come out of this is I have perfected the handbag-outward arm swing and am truly knowledgeable about meterage and space. I have a new community of "suspicious oldies" who can regularly lament to each other. I am winning. This is at least something new to talk about in our geriatric gatherings. We all feel the same way, and sometimes it's good to feel like one of the group.

JUST A THOUGHT

Suspicion is a heavy armor and with its weight it impedes more than it protects

– Robert Burns

SENIOR SAGE

Everything has a season, and we are in this season right now. Suspicion can turn its head rapidly, and people are most probably suspicious of you yourself, especially when turning up in a high-range prevention mask. Maybe it's a good idea to wear this protection everywhere as you will surely achieve your goal of absolute social distancing.

Ouch, I'm Seventy

AILMENT TALK IS CURRENTLY TRENDING IN OUR circles.

It seems everyone is now an expert in the discussion of retention of muscle tone and bowel movements. Everyone is so knowledgeable and experienced, and I am ready to run a mile.

Firstly, I don't like anything that is "icky" or "sticky". Then, of course, to balance out the other side, I devour medical almanacs like new release nonfiction.

But for fear of sounding tough, we are all becoming so experienced in ailments that I don't need to mirror my experiences with yours. I am fully trained already. Everything these days is invasive. Even the marauding threat of a deadly virus is invasive, so *stop*! There are more areas for our intellect to grow than discussion of lumps and bumps and blood results.

Oh dear, is this AWFUL?

I have a friend.

Social occasions with this friend are becoming difficult. We are quick off the mark to get to the restaurant first to manipulate the best Feng shui seating arrangements. Close proximity ensures an evening of grandchildren's poop or lack of it, the latest remedies for constipation, the skin freeze, the eye check, the heart murmur, the knee spasm, the… You catch my drift. Now, due to circumstances, we are sitting a distance apart, so there is a little buffer space, which I am joyfully embracing.

Then, I end the evening with neck strain, as I have spent most of the evening endeavouring to lean into the boy discussion at the other side of the table. American elections and Dow Jones and Everest climb talk is much livelier, and I just want to be a boy for the night so I can be part of the group. That sounds sexist, doesn't it, but… you get what I mean!

However, that conversation, I notice, is also beginning to deteriorate lately. Months of isolation and age creep have steered the conversation into cartilage problems and hearing deficit. Everyone at the table is now talking about wincing up stairs and investigating innovative pain relief injections and new procedures for knee-replacement operations. Everyone is now wearing their badge of honour—the latest compression bandage, where a little kneecap pops out to say a quick hello before it continues its greeting to the pavement.

On my side of the table, dinner companion is conversing in much more depth. Arrhythmia has crept into the conversation as she forgets to take a breath and the heart gives her a little reminder. Then the "I don't eat this as I think I am a coeliac," and "I don't eat that as I'm thinking of becoming vegan," and "I don't eat that because I loathe fish," and "I don't eat that as the salt increases my blood pressure," and "I don't drink that because I get migraines" and…

Well, why the f#%k have you come out for dinner? You may as well have stayed at home, sipped water, and watched the in-depth medical shows. You will truly be able to converse very eloquently and knowledgeably on all the other diseases that we could get because we are older.

I suppose it is time for us now to all be good patients and get out our home blood pressure monitors, and monitor …

Prick our fingers and check our sugars …

Find the contactless thermometers and take our temperatures …

Put ear wax remover in our ears…

Lubricate our eyes …

Rub in anti-inflammatory gel …

Take our acidophilus and vit C and D and prescription meds and herbal mixes …

Rub our trigger finger …

Locate our knee pillow …

And please, please, something to get us to sleep.

The day can't take any more of the ailment speak.

We are all spinning in a whirr of medications with side effects and medications for the side effect and medications for the side effect's side effect. "We are on a carousel, a crazy carousel," so says Jacques Brel.

A new community has sprung up now that we are on this side of the life scale. It is a community of sore speak, and I really don't want to be an inclusive member. I am only welcome, I understand, after seventy as I don't understand the language at entry level. I can only join this club when reaching the seventies starting line.

I'm not there quite yet, but I woke up this morning with a stiff neck and hullabaloo—I can now converse, I am an early adapter, I can become one of the group.

It is very exclusive, but I have a few referrals. I may be taken early if my ailments don't behave themselves.

It's the "Ouch, I'm Seventy" group, and soon, I suppose, I am going to be one of its very reliable and valuable members.

JUST A THOUGHT

"When you can't remember why you're hurt, that's when you're healed."

– Jane Fonda

SENIOR SAGE

Let's learn how to diminish the "sore." Let's speak positive affirmations and learn about medications and feed our bodies with simplicity and peace and stillness. Every part is connected. Let's work on making the whole feel so much better.

Get Your Advice from More Than One Source

"I AM SUSPICIOUS ABOUT THE MARK ON YOUR CHEEK."

Nobody likes to hear this on their annual visit to the general practitioner.

My GP is away on a well-deserved break, so I have popped into my local medical practice for a rapid once-over, after coffee with a friend recounting her horror stories of finds that turned out to be nasty. I don't want to delay any discovery of bits and bobs that may be growing insidiously somewhere on my torso.

"OK," I say, "so, what's next?"

"I need to make a little puncture in your cheek and send away for investigation," she replies.

I freeze for a second.

A hole in my cheek?

I have to think quick. I am a doctor's daughter, of course, so I am fully trained to question everything.

A hole in my cheek feels permanent. If I wanted permanence, I would surely have been rebellious and maybe added a little design, maybe a tiny little tattoo?

"I don't have time right now to do this procedure, but please book another appointment," she says.

I hotfoot out of the surgery to clear my brain. I don't know this doctor, and do I trust this diagnosis?

I challenge myself.

With an "ah, ah" in my gut, I dial my own GP's number and book an appointment post his vacation, knowing he will be well rested from his break and will give a well-informed diagnosis of the situation.

I am right. This mark is nothing. It receives a dose of cryotherapy, and I am good to go with my face perfectly intact.

♥

I had a blocked ear. It was so disturbing. I was so off balance. I needed help.

As I was out of town, it was again a quick visit to a local practice.

"How long has this been going on?"

"I'm not sure. It could have been for a week."

"Mmm." After looking in my ear, "I would like you to book in for a CT scan."

I go cold. A CT scan? Has the doc seen something unusual?

I put up with the balance issue. My family puts up with my narky mood and my plugged ears. I avoid the spontaneous suggestion of flying somewhere for a quick few days in the sun. Air flight and blocked ears are not good companions.

I visit my regular GP on my return, who syringes out the Rock of Gibraltar, and I am good to go.

My hacking cough is driving everyone mad. It is driving me mad as well. I don't feel well. Again, I land up in a strange medical practice where the locum doctor prescribes heavy cough suppressants and says all will be well. My gut says nah. I seek another opinion. This time from a rather alternative source but a doctor, nevertheless. I am sent off for immediate x-rays and diagnosed with pneumonia. If I had taken the cough suppressant I had been prescribed, who knows—I may not have been breathing at all.

I was dizzy for years. Blood work seemed OK. Investigations seemed OK. Diagnosis was anxiety. I didn't feel anxious. I withdrew. I was not myself.

I researched and educated myself on all causes of dizziness and took myself off to a bite specialist. It wasn't the last resort but was getting pretty close to getting there. With a slice of his drilling wand against a risen tooth that hadn't had a connection with any carbon paper on my last dental visit, my skull adjusted—*plonk*—into alignment, and within three days and some extra physio to calm the jangled nerves and muscles, I was right as rain. Anxiety? Puh-lease.

♥

And the famous final scene when my mum nearly had her leg amputated in error as the patient board hanging off the side of her bed in hospital had been replaced incorrectly. Another patient was sadly due to lose a limb that day. If it wasn't for her quick thinking, doctor's wife's instinct, to check and recheck, well, let's not even go there.

It seems like there is a lot going on in my health journal, but this is not so. I am perfectly healthy. These are simply examples as backup of my observations.

Thank God for doctors. They are miracle workers, and we are so appreciative of their skills. They save our lives and make us complete again. However, I always carry a level of suspicion with me into a doctor's waiting room. I remain observant of diagnosis and am practical and sensible in observance of what is absolutely necessary. I know medication is vital and lifesaving, but I turn a tablet over and over before swallowing, nervous of the treadmill of side effects that causes a Ferris wheel of further medication, a Ferris wheel that never backs up, a Ferris wheel that cannot stop, while pharmaceutical companies rub their hands in profitable glee.

If your gut is saying "ah ah," always check it out. Get your advice from more than one source, then make your decisions. Then, and only then, can you take full responsibility for the action from an informed and balanced point of view.

Something good has come out of this, however. I now read medical journals and alternative medicine articles like the latest best-selling novels. They intrigue me in their finds. I have become a veritable medical encyclopaedia.

Why didn't I become someone of significance in a medical field, I ask myself? Aah, now I know why, as I lightheadedly collapse onto the bed after viewing co-senior's bloodied stubbed toe.

JUST A THOUGHT

"If the world thinks you're not good enough, it's a lie, you know. Get a second opinion."

– Nick Vujicic

SENIOR SAGE

If you think about it, we could all be looking at the same thing, but our eyes never see this view from exactly the same place. We all have a different view. That sounds like life's lesson as well.

Our Hearts Are All the Same Colour

WE ALL HAVE A HEART.
Our hearts are all the same colour.
Think about this.
Think hard about this.
If your loved one's heart failed and they needed a new one, would you question the colour or culture or creed of the donor's heart?
Learn.
Educate yourself.
Evolve.
Become better.
We all deserve the same.
We are one.

JUST A THOUGHT

"No one is born hating another person because of the color of his skin or his background or his religion. People must learn to hate, and if they can learn to hate, they can be taught to love, for love comes more naturally to the human heart than its opposite."

– Nelson Mandela

SENIOR SAGE

"The world says fall in love, but the universe says rise in love."

– Matshona Dhliwayo

Trolling

CREATIVITY IS DAUNTING. PUTTING YOURSELF OUT there is brave.

Not many will take the risk.

Most fear failure.

Most are sensitive about criticism.

Most naively believe they are adored by all.

This is ***not*** so.

Expect the unexpected and toughen up.

Say hello to vulnerability, and enjoy the journey in faith despite fear. Faith and fear have something in common—you can't see either, so to move onwards and upwards, choose the positive version.

Public exposure will always draw in angry, bored, dissatisfied souls profusely seeking a target on which they can vent their own frustrations. Most won't attach a name to their poisonous rhetoric. Those who do are proudly polishing their badges in wait for an extra star on the ladder of "vitriolic comment" stardom. They want so badly to be noticed.

Don't notice!

Even the best of the best can be dumped in this melee of hateful comment. We all come out on the other side, quite intact, bringing wisdom, resilience and good humour into our constructive-criticism growth journal.

Take these as compliments, peeps. You have been noticed, and that is a good thing.

There is liberating freedom in understanding criticism that is constructive and criticism that is churlish.

I love the freedom in knowing who I am and moving past my own self-criticism. It has taken this long to let go, let loose and unapologetically be me. I now laugh at myself. I take no notice of venomous attacks and take joy in absorbing that which makes me better.

Take my advice, dear seniors—you also take no notice. It is only "them" who are hurting.

YOU are your own glorious YOU.

Step out and give things a go. It is so much more than nasty naysayers will ever do.

It is time, however, to take up the cudgel when comment is personal, intrusive, stalky or dangerous.

This is a different story.

This is *evil* "trolling", and we need to stand together to block this invasive vice that destroys victims' lives and sanity.

I remember trolls. Do you? – the little plastic dolls with colourful up-combed hair. Do you remember how we treasured and collected and swopped and searched for the good luck they would bring? Where have these little lucky charms vanished to?

Our little plastic dolls had names. Yet these trolls now remain nameless.

They are real, emotional troublemakers who poke at insecurities with their inflammatory and dangerous comments, waiting for reaction.

They endeavour to create hostility and conflict.

They love to see suffering.

They are cowards.

Where do they have the time to be so nastily persistent? How do they become so creative in their unsubstantiated remarks? A therapist would surely dig deep to discover some burgeoning scar of lack of identity or attention.

Trolling is insidious, nasty, personally invasive warfare. Do these ugly hidden faces know how they are affecting people? Of course, they don't care. They only want a reaction to be noticed. They poke and prod until they get one and leave a trail of devastation in their wake.

If you research, you will sigh at the long line of beautiful souls who have succumbed to these nameless bullies. It is heinous in its intention, and the guilty now in Australia could be trolling all their way to the courts.

I say be brave, not broken.

Read the good and the bad, and don't take much notice of either.

Never provide fuel for response.

These anonymous creeps will tire. Just remember, ***the dogs bark, but the caravan always moves on.***

JUST A THOUGHT

"If you're horrible to me, I'm going to write a song about it, and you won't like it. That's how I operate."

– *Taylor Swift*

SENIOR SAGE

The world is made up of all kinds. Mixed in between the lovely is the awful. Find your tribe. They will watch your back. In the end, good will triumph over evil.

Buy Memories, Not Stuff

MEMORIES AND MOMENTS, OH, HOW PRECIOUS YOU are to us as our gait and minds become slower.

What would you choose?

A laugh with a lonely friend or a set of Christofle silver cutlery? (*When are we going to use this? We don't entertain at home anymore, and there is too much cleaning up to do.*)

A meal with close friends and good company or a party on a yacht with gazillions of guests? (*We don't party on large boats anymore. We are nervous we may fall overboard in our lack of balance.*)

A swim in a calm clear ocean or a gold-studded, Chanel bathing suit? (*Oh my goodness, we don't want to draw any attention to ourselves now. We are quite happy in our black one piece.*)

A flight to explore the world or a set of Gucci luggage (*We travel light these days, and Gucci is popular with aspirational thieves.*)

A good night's sleep or a super-sized, new waterbed with all attachments (*There is only one form of waterworks these days, and it is not in the bed.*)

A Zoom chat with our grandchildren—well, nothing can compare with that, so I won't even try.

My thirteen-year-old motor vehicle or Elon Musk's Tesla (*Well?*)

Ongoing good health or a suite in a private medical centre. (*I don't think we want to go there, so get out your juicer quick smart and make an antioxidant concoction.*)

When all you have left is the memory of someone who has gone, then that memory will become one of your greatest treasures.

Let's go out and create more memories, seniors. They will feed our souls and feed those who recall them when we are long gone.

JUST A THOUGHT

"A man is made of memories. It is all we are. Captured moments, the smell of a place, scenes played out time and again on a small stage. We are memories, strung on storylines—the tales we tell ourselves about ourselves, falling through our lives into tomorrow."

– Mark Lawrence

SENIOR SAGE

"Sometimes you will never know the value of a moment until it becomes a memory."

– Dr Seuss

The Elbow Rock

CO-SENIOR AND I ARE BUSY, AND THEN WE ARE bored in this "iso" lockdown. So, we have donned our thinking caps to figure out a reward at the end of this period of extreme focus.

I engage in a "virus check" of the deep, dark, mouldy storage area to ferret out a board game, the chess board, monopoly or even a puzzle that would add some zing to the boredom.

Unfortunately, there are a few absent ingredients. The 1,000-piece puzzle has lost a few pieces. It may have been easier at 957, but we need order right now, and we are out of control with missing pieces.

The cards have also met the same demise, and we have forgotten which parts were which in the chess set box, so our pickings are getting rather slim. *Pictionary* is still wrapped in plastic, and the kids haven't taught us how to play, so we are lost. We've been told about *Cards Against Humanity*, a party game for horrible people, and since we've been isolated for so long we are not quite sure whether we have become horrible. We will leave that one alone until we have a solid assessment from close friends.

The search continues. I can see the tip of a 1970s tap shoe. "Pick me! Pick me!" it is silently beckoning.

We acquiesce, and co-senior sits on the floor and buckles me in.

My feet feel cosy as they don't come in half sizes, so I had cleverly bought a half-size bigger.

Somewhere in my recollection, I remember there is a matching pair for co-senior. So, with a hoist up and a clickety-clack, I delve further into the shelf to find his masculine version. They are found, resting and nicely wrapped in spider-web gauze, and we engage in a shoe-to-floor drum solo to evacuate the poisonous squatters who are most adamant that this is their home.

Now that we have found the bits, it is time to exercise, in time, in formation and what we can remember. It doesn't come back easy. The cha-cha beat has changed. It seems via YouTube that we step offbeat now, and we find this rather challenging.

You Tube has its own problems One of us needs to press "play", and as we are in senior years, we can't remember past the first step. By the time we have paused and regrouped, it's time to go back to the beginning to start again.

In our relay between channel changer and dancing space, we are interrupted by the latest news break of ventilator statistics and recoveries and death. We are then spoken to sternly as to what participation is allowed in the "out" and in the "in". We are terrified into submission, complying to our children's pleas of "Do not exit", and we reaffirm that we will be virtuous senior citizens and remain indoors.

Co-senior and I alternate between the twists and turns of news of new critical cases and the twists and turns of our new steps.

But in this "Gemini" mindfulness, I realise that co-senior has been on a grocery run this morning, and despite the fact that he was gloved and masked on this outing, I'm not sure whether he remembered to de-robe on his return. I am now circling in stressed union with the love of my life with my nose nestled in his "I'm going out" T-shirt. Ah, so that's why I can't remember the steps.

I retract my arms in rapid release, almost like a turtle head retraction, and my cool daddy is no longer "Daddy Cool." Our new dance is developing creatively.

It is no longer the "Eagle Rock".

It is rather unusual but most current. We don't hold hands; we don't touch faces; we don't adjust glasses. We have our new bump-the-elbow move.

Our routine is nearing perfection, and we have given it a new name.

It is the glorious, perfected, socially distanced, inventive, new world "Elbow Rock".

JUST A THOUGHT

If you tried to give rock and roll another name, you might call it 'Chuck Berry'

-John Lennon

SENIOR SAGE

Just get up and move, seniors, if you can, or at least tap your toes in your chair or turn the music on loud if you can hear. It will remove all your worries and your woes, just for a moment.

Guilty Gifts and Regifts

ON MY BIRTHDAY A COUPLE OF YEARS AGO, WE invited a very close friend and others to dinner at our house to laugh about our experiences and forget about things for a while.

This friend has a delightful sense of humour, displayed most prominently in his choice of birthday gifts on these special occasions. There are no expectations of a birthday parcel arriving with him, but he always excels in his unique, unexpected, off-centre choices.

The last birthday was no exception.

I watched him negotiating our steep driveway with a bottle of red in one hand and a sizeable object in the other. The bush turkeys in the garden were alarmed, scattering rapidly.

In his hand was an enormous, colourful, lifelike statue of a rooster. Then, with absolutely no embarrassment, said friend announced loudly to all present, "Everyone needs a large cock!"

I was delighted with my new acquisition, as the bush turkeys had been vigorously digging up our garden and nesting in the mulch. They were prodigiously proliferating, and our garden was a mess, and netting and scarecrows were not working. So, a huge colourful cock would surely frighten them away.

Some conservative friends, who visited shortly after, were taken aback. We heard from local whispers that they thought we had gone all kitsch and "gnomey," and maybe it was time for them to find new friends.

The year flew by rapidly, and it was time to celebrate again when birthday time came around.

Our "rooster friend" was always included in the celebrations and once again arrived at the front door, this time carrying a teeny weeny little gift.

I was ready for a surprise.

I gingerly opened the parcel to find an object that I couldn't really define. It could have been a clamp or an unusual paperclip or some inventive gadget that I hadn't come across in my kitchenware shopping. And, not to appear uneducated and a bit dim, I rolled the piece around in my hand, and unauthentically thanked him profusely for his unusual gift and would be enjoying working out how to use it.

He observed with deadpan face and then roared in mirth. It was actually an object that he had found on the ground, somewhere in his outings and, knowing how intensely polite I was, was trying to catch me off guard to see how I was going to react. He knew I was a people pleaser and would thank profusely. He wanted to playfully rattle the cage.

When I caught onto his prank, I collapsed in mirth as did everyone else who was in on the joke, and another year went by with our friendship still firmly intact.

Now gifts are a funny thing.

There seems to be huge anticipation these days before birthdays. Lists are subtly forwarded, cataloguing various desires and needs. The size and cost of the gift seems to be measured against the level of love and adoration. If that were the true marker of love, though, I would have been sorely hurt when co-senior and my children dashed out to the local pharmacy on the eve of one of my birthdays to buy whatever they could find with a shiny exterior.

They purchased a foundation on the sale shelf for a completely different skin colour. This, matched with a manual-hired treadmill, was proudly produced on the morning of B-day. I felt more love that day in the handmade card, flowers from the garden and coffee in bed. Now that was true gifting and love.

There is a word of advice regarding the re-gifting drawer. This can cause lots of trouble.

My one friend's birthday present was the same gift I gave her last year. My note remained unnoticed, tucked between the cardboard wrapping. She had grown a year older, so I forgive her for the memory lapse. And let's think positive—we both must like the same things if we are playing gift ricochet, so maybe that is why we are compatible.

My re-gifting drawer is pungent in lavender. It contains all the soaps and lotions doing the rounds between school classrooms and hairdressers. I loathe soap; it makes me itch.

I know lavender is calming, but with a never-ending surrounding aroma, I feel totally zonked and can't wait to depart with a little lavender parcel to be popped into the neighbour's postbox just to say thanks for bringing in the bins.

Be careful if you are going to re-gift. Make sure all the parts are still present. One gift I received was minus attachments, and nobody could provide a receipt for replacement and return.

In the re-gift, receipts always evaporate into thin air.

Gifts come from the heart.

Gifts should be given with love and joy.

Never have any expectations.

A beautifully written card or a "I'll get the groceries for you" or an unexpected family Zoom get-together or a photo book of old memories is just as wonderful.

Memories are our thing now. We want to be spoilt with moments. Please, please, don't give us the gifts that didn't work for you. They won't work for us either, and you may be unlucky when you open your next birthday parcel and the re-gift pops out and says,…

"I'm back!"

JUST A THOUGHT

Anything that has real and lasting value is always a gift from within.

– Franz Kafka

SENIOR SAGE

Gifting is not a measurement of love. It comes in all forms and is so special in any of these forms if the motivation of giving is enveloped in love.

I'm Standing Right Beside You

COVID-19 HAS LIKELY TRIPLED THE DEPRESSION rate, according to a first-of-its-kind study from the Boston University School of Public Health. As published in the journal *JAMA Network Open* on September 2, 2020, the study finds that 27.8 percent of US adults had depression symptoms as of mid-April, compared to 8.5 percent before the COVID-19 pandemic.

We have been out of control in 2020, and it has been so awfully hard for some.

Do you have friends who live on their own?

Are they lonely?

Have you connected to say hi?

Are you lonely?

Have you reached out to someone to let them know?

Has a friend passed away and left their partner grieving?

Do you know anyone who is struggling financially and putting on a brave face?

Can you pay forward?

Are *you* struggling?

Have you reached out to someone to let them know?

Are your friends drinking more, can't sleep, suffering from anxiety?

Can you give them information to speak to experts?

Are *you* drinking more, sleeping less, and panicking?

Have you asked for help?

I have friends who are lonely. We are lonely sometimes.

I have a friend who has lost his wife to COVID and is lost and grieving.

I have a friend who is struggling financially day by day.

I have friends drowning in wine.

I have friends losing sleep in their anxiety.

There are experts out there who can help.

Encourage people to search for this, to ask around, to seek online assistance.

I am not an expert, but in the meantime…

Be brave.

There is always someone out there who will stand right beside you.

Don't be frightened.

We have all been stripped of the clutter in 2020, and most have a deep desire to make our lives—*your life*—matter.

JUST A THOUGHT

"If you know someone who's depressed, please resolve never to ask them why. Depression isn't a straightforward response to a bad situation; depression just is, like the weather."

– Stephen Fry

SENIOR SAGE

It's OK to say you're not OK.

A Healthy Mind Body and Soul

"*Kokoro* is well understood in Japanese, but difficult to explain in English,' says Yoshikawa Sakiko, director of Kyoto University's Kokoro Research Center. Conceptually, it unites the notions of heart, mind, and spirit: It sees these three elements as being invisible from one other. 'For example if we say, "She has a good kokoro," it means heart and spirit and soul and mind all together'" (Ephrat Livni, *Quartz*, April 6, 2017).

I love the above description but also like to add in a little extra "body" as well. It is hard work getting older and keeping the puzzle pieces of life together. We have to work at and be aware of all elements to feel rounded and complete. Our minds need continual replenishment. We forget and retain less, and it concerns us. Our brains feel vacuous and unintelligent sometimes, and we spend time studying to be more worldly outside our memories and stories. We don't want to battle to spell *dog*, and only find common ground in extreme knowledge of degenerative senior diseases. We don't want to sink into academic contagion-speak.

So, how can we improve? These are my tips after years of experience.

HINTS AND TIPS FOR THE BRAIN

Lumosity

Have you ever tried these brain games? This app has exercises in speed, memory, attention, flexibility, problem-solving and more. You can even dodge other vehicles and marauding bushes whilst driving a racing car at speed.

Sudoku

Nine numbers in nine squares that can drive you nuts. Try with a timer on; it will stress you but keep you sharp. Don't give up.

Dancing

You need to remember the steps. It is good for you. Find a YouTube class. Nobody is watching, and there's the added bonus of perving the ripped Brazilian dance coach.

Chess

Improves your brain function, memory and strategic thinking. Do you know that scientists claim that playing chess can improve mental age by up to fourteen years?

Puzzles

Spread the pieces out with abandon. Choose interesting subjects, even maps to tizzle your imagination and increase your geographical knowledge. Swop puzzles with friends who are also improving their cognitive ability. Warning—it can become addictive.

Bridge

No, it is not just a card game. It kept my Mum's generation alive. You have to think.

Books

Read, read, read, read and read. Learn how to download Kindle versions. You can find free Kindles in different promotions. Readers are leaders even in older age. That is, if you want to be.

Colour

Relax, and fill in the lines. You can create some oh so pretty momentoes. Your grandchildren could even treasure and frame them.

There is more, so much more.

Crosswords, *Scrabble*, learning a musical instrument, doing an online computer course, joining a book club, social interaction, studying history, mapping ancestry and the list goes on.

HINTS AND TIPS FOR THE BODY

Exercise

Of course, we know this one. Exercise is good for us. Walk, swim, use weights to build muscles. We need those muscles as we get older. We need to keep our balance and protect our knees and our necks. Pilates, yoga (chair yoga if necessary) Stretchhhh…

Manage

Blood pressure, cholesterol, sugar levels, healthy colons, healthy eyes, prostate checks, mammograms, pap smears, skin checks.

Have regular annual medical once-overs.

Keep prescription medications under control.

Quit smoking.

Limit alcohol.

Drink water

We don't have a healthy thirst response as we get older, so download a "drink a glass of water reminder" app on your phone to remind you to stay hydrated.

Eat

We surely know by older age what is good for us and what isn't. You know you feel all clogged and sluggish after a week of hamburgers, french fries, desserts and greasy grub. We know we need to eat fruit and vegetables and whole grains as they supply an abundance of vitamins and fibre.

We know that too much sugar and too much salt is bad for us and that it moves us towards Type 2 diabetes and blood pressure problems. We know tinned food and processed food is laden with salt. Always read the instructions on the packaging. Check out the sodium levels—you may be surprised. If you can't pronounce ingredients, give them a wide berth.

We know that eating large carbohydrate meals washed down with alcohol before bed will cause indigestion and reflux and no sleep—or we should know by now.

So, let's get healthy. Let's sparkle again.

These foods will help:

Salmon, dark green leafy vegetables, blueberries, dark chocolate (yippy) nuts, turmeric, green tea, apple cider vinegar and much more if you delve deep into healthy eating.

Keep these in mind when choosing your menus. I promise you will see clearly again, you will run upstairs again and you will feel alive again.

Oh, and by the way, wheat and dairy can make you snotty and achy and inflamed and block your ears. You think you have dodged a reaction, but sorry, it usually says hello twenty-four hours later. Somehow pineapple helps. This is what works for me; it may not work for you.

Sleep

Why does sleep evade some of us when we get older?

Make sleep regular—have a bedtime routine.

Never search for your phone in the middle of the night to check the time.

Never turn on the light.

Don't make the room too warm. Dress lightly and cover comfortably.

Keep a magnesium roll-on next to your bed if you wake up with a cramp.

Ensure your pillow works for the contours of your neck.

Invest in a good mattress that works right just for you.

Turn off all electrical current in the room—it can make you feel shaky in the morning.

Wear a splint if you grind your teeth. It helps your jaw relax.

Now this one is going to be controversial. I ditch the face cream at night. It smears all over the pillow and then rubs into my eyes, and I wake up thinking I have developed rapid-growth cataracts. This one is up to you. It is not bothering the elasticity of my skin, but it may yours, so your choice.

HINTS AND TIPS FOR THE SOUL

Stress

You really need to manage stress. It can cause all kinds of unpleasantness.

Unclog your heart.

Have warm baths floating in magnesium salts.

Breathe in lavender, relaxing and pure.

Meditate. If you don't know how, go to a class or follow someone chanting on You Tube.

Breathe in blue, breathe out red.

Breathe.

Do all that is included in the sections above.

Never let the sun go down on your anger.

Have a routine.

Walk.

Laugh.

Love.

Be grateful.

Be still.

Thank your Higher Being.

I really, really want you to come on this wonderful, healthy senior's life journey with me.

At this age, you are free to do what you want (mostly). You are not being selfish.

It means you can contribute to saving the world, step by step, by being healthy in mind, body and spirit and then giving back to those who are not.

Only if you want to, of course.

JUST A THOUGHT

"Your mind is a reservoir of potential; your heart an ocean of strength; your soul a well of talents; and your body a vessel of power."

– *Matshona Dhliwayo*

SENIOR SAGE

"Your mind is a weapon. Your heart is an asset. Your soul is a treasure. Your life is a jewel." (Matshona Dhliwayo)

I couldn't say it more aptly myself.

We Can Still Be Rebellious, Can't We?

WE ARE AT THE MOVIES, CO-SENIOR AND I, SIPPING Cabernet Sauvignon from a straw out of our water bottles.

We are not allowed to bring in our own drinks, especially not the big *A*. But we have, and we feel naughty, and it is fun.

Packed in the bottom of my handbag is the snack platter bought from the local deli.

"Hold this," I say to co-senior, handing him my laced water bottle.

"And don't spill, as they will smell us as they walk by and kick us out."

"Who cares?" chortles co-senior.

I like his spunk.

"They are going to kick out two seniors having a little fun? I don't think so. They are having a little inner giggle themselves. 'Thank goodness,' they say. 'We are not the only naughty ones imbibing in our parents' wine cellar while they are away.'"

I smile and recline into my seat, sipping and snacking and feeling very adventurous.

Our definition of adventure and rebellion, however, has changed now that we are older.

My father broke a hairbrush on my backside when I was a teenager for jumping on the back of a revved-up Ducati, with a revved-up, passionate Italian. His ripped muscles were far too hard to resist. It was kinda nice to hold on to them very tightly. So nice that I lost perception of time and arrived back at my family door to a puce-faced father—surgeon father—who had called every hospital emergency department to see if a broken young woman had been delivered into their healing hands.

I know, I know. I did *say* I would never ride on the back of a motorcycle, but I didn't *promise* not to, so I didn't break a promise. I never break promises.

I forgave my dad after the torture of walking through a ward of his young patients who had lost limbs in their rebellious drunken adventures.

But now that I am older, I like the term *constructive nonconformity*.

I don't want to be on the sideline watching others being less fearful of stretching the rules.

Francesca Gino, a professor and researcher at Harvard Business School, researches people who engage in this constructive nonconformity. She asserts that "the future belongs to the rebel, to those who break rules, who question situations and dare to think differently."[1]

I do like the different thinking aspect, but maybe rules are there for our protection. I take cognizance of this and am, I must admit, a bit of a goody-goody in being careful not to stretch the bar too far.

We are not all having midlife crises; we are having midlife *opportunities.* We don't really have to prove ourselves to anyone but our own free selves.

A little inner rebellion will do us no harm. Let's admit it. This is the first time in a very long time we can say and do what we really, really want with no reprisal. Our excuse can always be old age.

Does getting older make you feel so liberatingly emancipated?

I hope so, and the feeling of rebellious freedom sort of feels *oh so good.*

JUST A THOUGHT

"Other people will call me a rebel, but I just feel like I'm living my life and doing what I want to do. Sometimes people call that rebellion, especially when you're a woman."

– Joan Jett

SENIOR SAGE

I feel so free questioning the status quo if it doesn't feel quite right. I won't buck the rules unless they are obviously unfair, and then I will be extremely rebellious in questioning any wrong or injustice that needs to be righted. You too?

We Are Just Passing Through

WHEN WE SEE EVIDENCE FROM AUTHORITATIVE scholars that aliens have been sighted and they could possibly be a "thing", it makes one think, doesn't it?

This whole thought process started on my morning cycle (not out-in-the-fresh-air cycle but steadfast on my stationary bike). The gauge of how much I love my exercise for the day is based on the latest book I have discovered. If it is a winner, I can voraciously absorb and forget that the muscles in my legs are mimicking a"Peloton" party covering great distances on the dial.

But today I am distracted by my book.

I am doing so very well until I read that we have a birth date (yes, we can plan for that) and a death date (no, we can't plan for that), and it is all written in our very own personal book of life. So, in conclusion, we are just "passing through".

I screech to a halt, as suddenly my to-do list and grocery trip and sore toe is now so very irrelevant and unimportant.

So, if these aliens are, pretty promise, not part of a psychedelic experience, and the *Guardian* reports on 27 April, 2020, "the Pentagon on Monday released three declassified videos that show US navy pilots encountering what appear to be unidentified flying objects," then it is time to sit up and take notice.

I delve into past records and read stories about many pilots spotting weird objects and shapes in our expansive sky. We may not know the real numbers of these sightings. Pilots may have kept this in their personal memory banks for fear of being labelled "cuckoo" with possible retrenchment and annihilation of their careers.

We also know there are extremely efficient photoshopping experts who can turn the Loch Ness Monster into a flying dinosaur, and some in their eagerness embrace these formations with eager belief.

My co-senior—my *conservative* co-senior—spotted a UFO when he was seventeen. He has never wavered from his story. Even fifty years later, it is distinct in its detail.

He looked up in the sky and saw a very bright, round object with flares around the bubble shining intensely above his head. It hovered and hovered and hovered, and then—swoosh—it catapulted into the black of the night.

Co-senior was not blinded by the effects of the seventies and always speaks his truth. He is my conservative co-senior, as I explained. It would be extremely difficult for him to embellish a story.

He also, at the age of eight, was enveloped by a supernatural light of liquid love. Abstract, unexplainable, inexplicable, complete.

He ran and jumped into bed between his parents. They comforted and loved him for the lack of explaining the unexplainable.

Co-senior is connected to something that is not earthly. The light shines on him. He sees the light.

Are these singular human beings who have sighted weird objects just as reliable as co-senior?

This is not "woo-woo".

There is something out there we are desperately trying to understand.

Some of us are brought up in a faith.

Let's take as an example the Christian faith, where we believe "for God so loved the world, that He gave His only begotten Son, that whoever believes in Him should not perish but have everlasting life" (John 3:16).

Does this mean that God is also extending this promise to those who may inhabit other planets who are not like us but still have the ability to think, analyse and believe? And how far away are these planets? And last thought—are there others who look like us who inhabit other planets?

We do have some pretty extraordinary brains in the world, so is there a way we can communicate with the "others" in a cross-educational verbal form? Sort of like the guy who learned how to speak "magpie" to prevent magpies from their attacking swoop as he innocently rode by. (This is a thing in Australia.)

So now, we are passing through…..

Does this mean we are passing through to become higher beings on another faraway planet with humans who look just like us but have hugely superior brains?

Whoever these aliens may be, they have worked out how to have a little "looky looky" at us, their faraway brothers. We earthlings are looking their way too. We are observing all planets we can see through our Gran Telescopio Canarias, the largest optical telescope in the world.

This home on earth is simply temporary.

When we look back as seniors, it seems to have gone in a blink. But it is only momentary, and we can either make it incredible and magnificent and inspiring and educational and loving and spiritual and death-defying, or reach the end as an insignificant blip.

We will pass through the bubble to the other side and to who knows where.

In the meantime….

Let's live in the moment, dear seniors.

Let's make the absolute best of the temporary.

We will all know the answers when we climb through the clouds at the top of the Faraway Tree (Enid Blyton). When we peek through, I am sure there will be an amazing eternal discovery right there, just waiting for us on the other side.

JUST A THOUGHT

"We are just passing through. Our purpose here is to observe, to learn, to grow, to love—and then we return home."

– Australian aboriginal proverb

SENIOR SAGE

If this life is just about a temporary passing through, we better be sure that, whatever our circumstances, we need to be living in this very moment. For those who believe this is all there is, I would make the very, very most of it, as this is your one and only chance.

Flattening the Curve

WE WERE INITIALLY CONFUSED WITH THE WORD *corona* as it used to mean a good "stubbie" (the crown of beers), on a Saturday night. Now we have a double entendre, and we don't want to be anywhere near the word in one of its forms.

Manufacturing entrepreneurs are rubbing their hands in glee, endeavouring to keep up with mask demand while raking in the dollars. It's all become fancy-schmancy with designs and imprinted phrases: "You are too close" or "Stop staring, where's your mask?"

We now know what a respirator does and pray that we don't need one to keep us breathing.

And we are advised to sit tight to flatten the curve.

We are all certainly flattening the curve in our own way. We are developing our new "flattening the curve" large and expansive derrieres, firmly attached to a "very bad for your posture" chair. Flesh is expanding, like an overfilled chicken pie. The chairs seem to be getting smaller, and our body parts are seeping slowly and horizontally between the armrests and towards the opposite walls.

Will our silhouettes ever be the same again?

We understand social distancing. We practiced it in our junior days when Mr full-of-himself jock threw unkind comments at our adolescent insecurities while exposing his own extreme halitosis affliction. Social distancing was pleasant then and actually most welcome. We knew our meterage then, putting us in good stead now.

Of course, we are all very aware that these measures are absolutely necessary, and we hiss at those who have decided they are impervious to germs and congregate in groups with their Coronas in hand, spreading the silent-form corona unawaredly between themselves. We are stuck between feeling naughty and "what the hell", as surely a cough from a way away is not going to destroy our lungs.

But then, on our Morning News Show, the resident doc advises that a cough could travel so much farther than we think and it is better being in front of a person than behind if there is an emission, as droplets seem to travel in this direction. We are informed that these same droplets can jump over a few aisles in a supermarket hitting the innocents silently grabbing their Lindt bars to assist in their boredom.

But back to flattening the curve. My trousers are not comfortable and are happy that they are also in isolation at the moment as the seams are taking a battering. Unfortunately, while observing all mandates by government bodies, my body is now "fattening the curve" and is blooming in body opulence.

Thank goodness for co-senior, who always felt he would have lived very comfortably in the Baroque era and thinks his one and only *babushka* is truly Rubenesque delicious.

JUST A THOUGHT

Real women are fat. And thin. And both and neither and otherwise.

SENIOR SAGE

Keep your pantry as healthy as you can—it will serve you well in the future. And obviously a little breakaway into yummy snack world is A-OK. If you feel like it, have it, just one little piece at a time.

Pecking Order

THERE IS A CACOPHONY OF SOUND OUTSIDE MY window.

Two rosellas have discovered the blazing red bottlebrush bush, and they are having so much fun nibbling and springing amongst the leaves. Sometimes I can't locate them as their colour blends harmoniously in the red and green, and then suddenly—whoosh—they appear resplendent in variegated colour and joyfully swing upside down between the branches.

It is inspiration for a painting—if only I could paint.

I have a thing about birds.

When my dad died, a bird tapped on the window next to his bed, all day and all night, as he peacefully slipped away. It was persistent in its inclusion in this supernatural moment. And then, at last breath, it simply stopped and flew away.

That night as I lay in bed, with thunder and lightning ending the day in its crescendo, a single bird stepped forward through the booms and flashes and chirped incandescently through the clamour. I was awake, sad in my extreme loss. I listened to this single voice trying to reach out to me in my sorrow. It was pouring rain yet this single bird was chirping and interpreted as "Julie, I'm here. Julie, I'm here."

A friend of my friend was ill, extremely ill, hospitalised ill. She lay in recovery in a hospital on an extremely high floor of a recuperation complex.

A low-flying species of bird sat on the windowsill every day, seemingly spurring her on to recovery. It never wavered in its companionship; it was just there. The day she departed the ward and moved onwards to a new, healthy life, the bird flew away. It was never seen on that windowsill again.

The two rosellas today in my garden have claimed their tree space and are effortlessly stripping the branches of their flowers.

But they are not happy.

A kookaburra has settled on a leafless branch close by. This bird is big. It glances from left to right, surveying the skittish birds on its right but also keeping a close eye on my face, staring out of the window on the other side. A swarm of bees are buzzing too close, and they are telling them to "buzz off."

They are all defending their playground. The best way they know is with shrill noise. Down below, magpies are nonchalantly striding, seeking or defending their own trees. Spring has sprung, and they are on alert to swoop and terrorise those they fear or faces they remember and simply do not like.

The little rosellas are growing louder in their defence. This is their tree, and they are defending vigorously. Aware of the bigger predator below, they spread their wings and "bird talk" their supremacy.

I am watching them stand their ground.

They are not fussed by my presence, and when I open my window to mimic their bird call, they peek curiously in my direction to see if I am worth the attention.

I get back to writing, and the noise settles. I look up, and the rosellas are now sitting on the windowsill before me. They quizzically tilt their heads, greeting me in their own personal way. I reach out my hand to the pane of glass. They are not frightened. They hop and nuzzle and tweet and simply say hello.

I swear this is my mum and dad. They are simply checking into my awareness with rainbows of light.

"Hello," I answer.

A dove appeared at the baptism of Jesus. Why a bird? It is said that this was the Holy Spirit descending on Jesus in another form.

These beautiful creatures are messengers of God, I believe. They bridge the gap to what we spiritually wish to understand. Our loved ones are watching us always.

"Hello, rosellas, you have revived my personal lineage."

Maybe one day I may also be frolicking with you amongst the glorious colours of the bottlebrush tree.

JUST A THOUGHT

"I pray to the birds because I believe they will carry the message of my heart upward. I pray to them because I believe in their existence, the way their songs begin and end each day—the invocations and benedictions of Earth. I pray to the birds because they remind me of what I love rather than what I fear. And at the end of my prayers, they teach me how to listen."

– Terry Tempest Williams in Refuge: An Unnatural History of Family and Place

SENIOR SAGE

Stay still, observe and listen. There is so much we do not know but so much we can learn.

"Therefore I tell you, do not worry about your life, what you will eat or drink; or about your body, what you will wear. Is not life more than food and the body more than clothes? Look at the birds of the air, they do not sow or reap or store away in barns, and yet your heavenly Father feeds them. Are you not much more valuable than they? Can any of you by worrying add a single hour to your life? (Matthew 6:25–27)

Letter to My Grandchildren

If you don't have grandchildren, you may not relate to this chapter. You may have other little people in your heart who are not blood grandchildren but hold a special place in your heart. Then this chapter will be for you. If not for you, we can meet up again in the next chapter.

TO MY DARLING LITTLE LOVED ONES,

I have commenced the workday, sitting at my desk. Perched on the ledge, just to the right of me, glinting in my peripheral vision, is "our" treasure trove. You know which one I mean. It is filled with all our shared delights. These are not things; these are our memories. These are the memories that only you and I can fill.

Your sparkly sequined bag takes pride of place in the corner. As the spring sun beams through the window, it catches a sequin in its ray and projects a rainbow on my cheek. I feel you. I feel you when you hide this in my suitcase when we left your home to fly to ours across the sea, and I feel you when it shouts "Surprise!" as I unpack my well-worn clothes. We have a "pretty promise", you and I, that we will hand over this treasure to each other every time we meet so that we both hold a bit of each other in our hearts when we are not together.

Next to your bag is Koyan. We found him under the sofa when we at last got to mopping the floor. You taught us about your favourite *Lion King* movie, and we watched Mufasa's death a thousand times together, wrapped in each other's arms on the couch. You recite the scene verbatim, even though you are still so very little. You told me when we spoke today that there could be some changes to this story. Wow! Does that mean we will cuddle together another thousand times? I can't wait.

There is a pink, spiky, fluffy ball and a button and a painted rock and your first drawing and a picture of Mummy and Daddy and your baby sister and Gagga and Pappa and four dogs all blended together. I love that picture; it means family.

Oh, and I forgot your squishy bird that lights up when you press the rubber tummy. We had to discard the light before getting on the flight as we didn't know whether batteries were safe or not. But that's OK—we can use Pappa's reading light when we are next together.

I know your face when you are sad or frightened. I love that you know exactly where my number is on Mummy and Daddy's phone if you just want to say hi or need us in an emergency. I will always pick up when you dial. I am so grateful you are my blood. You are mine, and I am yours.

We are one.

♥

Your piercing blue eyes touch mine. You tell me that you love me so, so, so, so much, and your little body moulds into mine as I read you stories and you drink in the words. You think I am sort of a boy because I understand Transformers and Bots and Cars. This is a great compliment.

I haven't told you that I have secretly watched all your TV shows so I can communicate in your language.

You spread out your mealtimes so we can collapse laughing and love deeply. You are fast becoming a Messenger special effects expert. I am fast becoming a unicorn or an alien. You are so like your daddy when he was little. I am overjoyed that I now have more time to just be with you. When Daddy was little, it was oh so much harder. You make my heart dance, and I wait for the moments when I can pick you up and throw you in the air and hear your guffaw. You are mine, and I am yours.

We are one.

My beautiful rainbow baby.

You are all that our family needed when it was time to need. I know your smell of familiarity and birth blood. You slept in my arms for eternity, nestled into my neck wrinkles. You knew I was yours, and you were mine.

Your curls are your great grandmother's, your mumma's and mine—same face, same depth, same loving. You know my name on Facetime and shout it out proudly. We are forever connected. I watch your mannerisms and feel like I have known you before. You feel like my mum, and that makes me feel safe. I feel she has returned to love again. You are the same star sign. You stroke my face and kiss my lips through the barrier of distance. You know you are loved even though we are separated. We will create our own life stories when we are together again. I want to feel your soft skin and see your piercing eyes and grow up and grow old together. Soon, very soon, my precious one. You are mine, and I am yours.

We are one.

♥

Your eyes are a twinkle. Your bow is in your hair. Your tulle twirls, and your handbag completes. Today you are only one. You know who you are and where you are going. You already know that we love you right down deep in our hearts. You make us laugh. You do extraordinary things for a little girl who is so little. You are smart and gentle and good and calm and good for us all. You understand me, and I understand you, both loving each other deeply. Your beautiful face smiles peacefully. You are still so very little, but you smile at our names and connect with our brains. You will change the world, my little angel. You are mine, and I am yours.

We are one.

♥

And to grandchildren who are all grown up. You are also in our lives, and we will get to know you and hear your stories when you are inquisitive about your ancestry. We have enough love to go around; you just need to come and find it.

JUST A THOUGHT

"Grandchildren: My favorite hello and my hardest good-bye."

– Unknown

SENIOR SAGE

Grandparents connect children to their roots. Sometimes there are "grandies" out there who we adopt into our hearts. There is always a Gagga and Pappa out there for those who don't have any. We have enough love to share around. We can also be your home.

Do What Works For You

We are all one day older every day. If we understand that, our lives could possibly become so much richer.

We all have opinions, and our opinions sometimes differ and that is healthy.

We are all trying to do our best. Some of us try to do better, and that becomes our best.

We are all human and make mistakes.

We all have the capacity to love.

We all can feel lonely and isolated.

We all cry. We all poop. We all laugh.

We discover strategies that work for us as we grow older. Some of the strategies that work for me won't work for you.

That's OK.

So here is what I hear, read, digest and work out for my so-called best life:

Eat bananas; they are packed full of potassium.

Don't eat bananas as you will look like an "apple".

Hit the aerobics classes; it keeps your heart healthy.

Don't hit the aerobics classes; it will damage your knees.

Eat cauliflower, it helps you lose weight.

Don't eat cauliflower; it messes with your thyroid.

Vaccinate; it will save your life.

Don't vaccinate; viruses mutate, so you won't be protected.

Move into a retirement village; you will feel so safe.

Don't move into a retirement village; keep your independence.

Are you confused? Mmm. So am I.

STOP

Take a breath and think through your own list, not tampered or tainted or influenced, just yours—what actually and authentically works for you.

Here are some ideas that work for me.

- Develop a routine. Structure is productive.
- Make your routine enjoyable.
- Start the day with a hot or warm drink.
- Coffee is my thing, but yours may be water and a squeeze of lemon juice.
- Read a passage from your book of faith.
- Write down three things for which you are grateful.
- Dig deep and stay still or meditate, or whatever *you* call it, before the world explodes around you.
- Stretch or walk or exercise.
- Massage your lymph nodes—it disperses extra fluid.
- Eat a healthy breakfast.
- Include blueberries.
- Take a warm shower with a final burst of cold.
- Take necessary vitamins, probiotics and prescriptions.

- Do sudoku.
- Don't stress if you need to do all this before work (if you work).
- Write out your goals for the year.
- Write out your goals for the month.
- Write out your goals for the week.
- Write out your goals for the day.
- Tick the goals off your list when done.
- Write down the phone calls you need to make.
- Write what you need to do out of the house.
- Write what you need to do inside the house.
- Do the nasty stuff up front.
- Pay any bills straight up so they don't spoil your day.
- Practice an instrument if you are learning one.
- Batch cook and freeze.
- Become a student—keep learning.
- Keep up with technology.
- Drink water—*drink lots of water.*
- Do washing once a week.
- Keep your bedroom tidy and your bed made.
- Keep your kitchen tidy and your counters clean.
- Get rid of items you don't love, need or to which you have no emotional attachment.
- Always pick up the phone when your grandchildren call.
- Never pick up the phone when there is NO ID.
- Learn to say *no.*
- Make new friends.
- Join new communities.
- Map out your money.
- Walk down the stairs one step at a time.

- Check that all the plugs are turned off before going out.
- Wash the channel changer after working with chicken.
- Keep your password book in a safe place.
- Cold pool water helps with the aches.
- Be you, and be comfortable being authentic you.
- Love yourself.
- Always pack *your mask* (that is today, of course, and may not be forever).
- Move.
- Donate.
- Un-retire!

Do not fear change. If fears arise, meet these fears face to face. Stare them down, face them head on. Most of what we fear never eventuates. Find your place of calm, the ocean, your familiar chair, a walk, within.

- *I choose peace*
- *I am calm, happy, and content*
- *I have power to create positive change*

Do not fear loss of control. There are certain elements of our lives that we can control. Habits and routines keep us in control.

- *I am in control of how I react to others*
- *I am in charge of my life*
- *Negative thoughts only have the power I allow them*

Do not fear lack of identity. Build up your sense of self. Make yourself strong. Write and repeat positive affirmations about yourself. Believe you are great and still have so much to offer.

- *I am worthy of love*
- *I approve of myself and love myself deeply*
- *My imperfections make me unique*
- *My potential is limitless*
- *My life becomes richer as I become older*
- *I make a difference to people around me*
- *I am happy*

Life moves through seasons. If this is our winter, then spring eventually comes. Choose to be happy and hold onto hope. It will serve you so well in the long run.

JUST A THOUGHT

"Aging is an extraordinary process where you become the person you always should have been."

– David Bowie

SENIOR SAGE

Unwrinkle your heart, not your body. Fill your heart with compassion, empathy, happiness and, most of all, love.

Be Someone for Someone

WE HAVE LEARNED SO MUCH ABOUT OURSELVES in 2020.

We have learned that we are resilient.
We have learned we are fragile.
We have attempted new skills and studied courses online.
We cry silently at the lack of living close to our children and grandchildren.
We treasure simplicity.
We breathe open air, first time for a long time.
We talk, and we listen.
We hear our families. We heal our families.
Our families hear us.
We say we are sorry.
Our vision of life is clearer.
Our vision of life is more unclear.
We see the end in sight.
We don't see the end in sight.
We are frustrated.
We are contented.
We are angry.
We are scared.

We are sad.

We are lonely.

We have learned to submit.

On opening my eyes this morning, I observed co-senior sitting upright on his side of the bed. He was dressing quietly so as not to wake me. I lay still and continued observing. He was unaware of my open eyes watching every move.

After a while, once fully dressed, he simply sat peering out of the window, observing the dawning of another day. He was still, his eyes drinking in the blended, pastel masterpiece of the morning sky. My heart was full but sad.

I reminded myself that it was my responsibility to keep us both healthy to ensure that we could experience so many more of these beautiful dawns.

I reminded myself that two could become one.

What would happen if our beautiful, gentle pastel colours became a lackluster monochrome?

What would happen if we peered out of that window and absolutely nobody was observing us?

There are numerous stories we read about desperate loneliness after the death of a partner. Some sink into oblivion, and others plead for companionship.

Do you know that 35 percent of seniors spend Christmas alone or isolated?

Some try and sleep the day away saying it's just another day. Yet others become inventive.

An elderly man in the UK, who had lost his wife from cancer, launched an appeal for someone to be a guest in his home and eat Christmas dinner with him. With a promise of good food, good company, and good wine, he couldn't face being on his own at this time. The unremitting silence was torturous. He desperately needed company.

Imagine the desperation in having to appeal to a stranger for Christmas day companionship?

My heart and instinct is soulfully receptive to the cry.

Christmas Day is meant for celebration and yet can be so sad.

I personally invite all who do not have a place, to *my* home to celebrate, when I can. We are a mixed, eclectic bunch but are all so similar in our human desire to belong and to share and to love.

We are so fortunate to be alive. We need to share this fortune to help keep others afloat.

Have *you* been someone for someone in 2020?

Have you shared the love that you have.

The world is changing, and our conscience is poked to be better.

We can be oh so good moving forward.

Let's just do it.

Let's be connected to love and hope and companionship.

It can only feed the soul.

JUST A THOUGHT

The best thing about the worst time of your life is that you get to see the true colours of everyone.

SENIOR SAGE

Look outward, not inward. It is so healing for others but especially for yourself.

Photo Opportunity

When Mumma is wrist deep in kneading dough and skimming consommé, her boy cub and I have a nightly routine.

His Pavlovian "speak to Gagga" response kicks in.

Tonight, he has much to tell. It is time for Gagga to be lectured on the new toy that is "more than meets the eye." This little one is so smart. With Rubik's Cube-like rapid movement, his little fingers shift from vehicle to action figure and back to vehicle in the blink of an eye.

I am engrossed.

"Oh, my goodness, you will have to teach Gagga," I expound with enthusiasm.

With that, every Transformer he owns finds a place in the transformation queue. Beware if my eyes linger on anything other than full attention.

"Gagga, Gagga, watch. Watch."

"Transforming" is not his only skill.

He has now found the "home button" on his mumma's phone and, with shrieks of laughter, has worked out that if the button is pressed continuously while we are speaking, he will have a keepsake of Gagga's contorted face a gazillion times on Mumma's screen. I am very grateful that his mumma and I have a very good relationship as a mother-in-law's face staring back day and night could become one step further than challenging.

Boy cub has now moved up a class. He knows how to press the Antarctic Blue whale that has been assigned to Gagga's number. I am not sure how to take this but decide to take the complimentary route when I learn that they have big hearts. I am unsettled with the label of "loudest animal on the planet" and "tongues as big as an elephant".

Despite my new avatar, I am delighted that I am accessible at any time. He is delighted too. I now receive calls from the Zoo or a swimming lesson or when charading as Iron Man inside a cardboard box.

I remind myself that bathroom calls need to be handled with care. The images between these walls do not have a PG rating.

Our communication is progressing well until things took an unusual turn last night.

Mumma was in the shower, and Mumma's phone was taking a break on her bedside table. This was in full view of little cub who angelically waited to hear the whoosh of water before grabbing and endeavouring to sneak in a little "Bluey" time.

This was not working in his favour.

"Mummy, are you finished yet? Mummy, are you finished yet? Mummy, are…"

In frustration, his fingers are pounding on the "0" button, hoping to unlock whatever is locked for him to sneak in a "watch" before mumma is dry.

At this stage, there is some connection confusion. He believes that Gagga will be a comforting element to curb his rising exasperation.

"0-0-0-0-0-0-0-0-0-0-0-0-0"

"You have dialled emergency Triple Zero. Your call is being connected."

"Oh, Gagga, your voice sounds funny."

"Do you need police, fire and rescue or ambulance?"

"No, Gagga, you know I have Barricade and Inferno and Autobot Ratchet. Don't be silly, Gagga. I've got them already."

"Which state are you calling from?"

"Oh, Gagga! I'm home, Gagga, I'm home!"

"Are you OK, bubs?" Mumma calls out from the shower.

"I'm OK, Mumma."

"Is your Mumma all right?" continues the operator.

"Can you call your mumma?"

"Mumma!" shouts little cub.

Mumma doesn't reply as she is enjoying washing off layers of stress from a busy week.

Boy cub knows the red "end" button, presses and capitulates to regrouping with his beloved Transformers.

The phone rings.

Boy cub presses "end."

The phone rings.

Boy cub presses "end".

The phone rings.

Mumma is finished with her shower. She rushes to answer.

"This is 000. Did you call?"

"Um, no" says Mumma.

"Do you need help? Please confirm you don't need help."

"Oh, I am so sorry," says Mumma, "It must have been my little boy."

"Please confirm that you don't need help."

With a firm admonishment from all sides, the situation is resolved.

But, one day *you* may need emergency help.

Do you know what to do? Have you a system in place?

The systems will be different in different countries.

Learn what you need to do to receive immediate assistance in the case of an emergency.

We all think we are omnipotent.

Not so!

We are in slip, trip and fall territory.

I know this, as a while back I slid across the wet bathroom-floor tiles and fractured three ribs in my haste. My emergency go-to was my knight-in-shining armour, who arrived speedily on the scene. He was a medic in the army so I was in safe hands.

You may not be so lucky, so set up emergency contacts in your phone *today*.

One day it may just be *your* emergency.

JUST A THOUGHT

Be strong enough to stand alone, smart enough to know when you need help and brave enough to ask for it.

– Ziad K. Abdelnour

SENIOR SAGE

From the moment you realise there is an emergency, that is the moment you never panic.

Simplicity

ISOLATION HAS RETURNED US TO SIMPLE.

It has torn back the layers of freneticism and has centred our souls on what, after all, is most important. No greed or ambition or jealousy or competition; simply health and peace and safety and connection and love.

And that simply is what all human beings at base level would surely want or need, is it not?

When we peer dubiously around the corner and into a possible new way of life, will it be the same life or unrecognisable from everything we once knew? Will we be so changed that we don't even crave what we had before?

Some expound loudly that they are bored and frustrated and demotivated and depressed, and they are. But there is a large secret ballot of us who love being at home and hope that the status quo may remain for a little while longer in the future. We have adjusted to the new way and at last comprehend that some aspects of our previous life were not as satisfying as we believed.

This of course excludes a large percentage of frazzled parents of young children who have had to quick smart become experts in all fields of education. And those who are not that connected who now endure rivers of anger flowing between them as they defensively wait for the banks to burst.

Home is a jumbled conglomeration of life, mixed with work, mixed with education. It is messy.

We submit or challenge. It is peaceful or chaotic. It is joyful or frustrating. It is our choice alone.

Simplicity makes it easier.

We can simplify our homes and become more minimalist.

We can simplify our closets with only outfits that we love.

We can simplify accessories and give them away.

We can simplify technical intrusion by limiting to certain times of day.

We can simplify calls by not answering the phone.

We can simplify food by eating fresh and healthy with uncomplicated recipes.

We can simplify friendships by not trying too hard with relationships that don't work.

We can simplify exercise routines by walking in the sun and floating in the sea.

We can simplify lists.

Start a simple list:

- What is important?
- What can be done later?
- What is a whim?

Deleting the whims will become wins.

Try this little test.

Look at your list for the month (if you have one), and write down what doesn't really need to be done on a separate piece of paper.

Buy a filing tray, and mark it pending.

Put this removed list into the pending tray.

Forget about the list.

Revisit the list after one month. Is there a possibility there is nothing on that list you needed to do?

….and you have been carrying around this baggage in your stress basket for how long?

With less to do and more simplicity, we have more time. We all want more time. It is our most valuable commodity.

There is more time to listen and more time to talk.
There is more time to create.
There is more time to rest and sleep.
There is more time to meditate and pray.
There is more time for healthy living.
There is more time for connection.
There is more time for spirituality.
There is more time for creativity and learning.
There is more time to laugh.
There is more time to love and be loved.
There is more time to notice and to breathe.
There is more time to give back.

Simplicity does not make you limited.

In fact, in the words of Lao Tzu, simplicity is the ultimate sophistication.

JUST A THOUGHT

“The greatest step towards a life of simplicity is to learn to let go.”

– Steve Maraboli, Life, the Truth and Being Free

SENIOR SAGE

Oh, how I love how I breathe in simplicity. I hear my breath—in and out—and my mind is still to face the onslaught of the challenges we observe every day.

Don't Get Sucked into a Scam

TRILL, TRILL.

The home phone is ringing, and it is unusual.

Nobody I know uses a home line. We do, as the installers inform us that this line is connected to the internet.

And we need the internet.

Four shiny handsets are dotted around the house creating panic when all four emit their shrill scream when somebody dares to call, and we run laps around the house trying to remember where these four units have been placed.

We have, however, been introduced to a new intruder checking up on us every day.

We never answer as we don't feel safe. The intruder's name is "Anonymous." Sometimes our curiosity gets the better of us, and we submit.

We have recently entered a television channel's "cash cow" competition and maybe, just maybe, it is our lucky day to bury our credit card debt and dream about cocktails in the Maldives.

I pick up. There is a mumble and a fumble on the other side. There is background chatter and echo (a good sign) and then a rapid unintelligible greeting in an unintelligible foreign accent.

After I listen to a hasty introduction, I am advised that my NBN connection is about to disappear into the clouds, and if I don't react on the spot, it is likely I will never be part of the new tech order ever again.

I wasn't to be frightened as said caller would clearly walk me through the steps to ensure that all would be "good in the hood". All I need to supply is my licence number, ID, banking details and passwords and anything else I may have that will prove who I am.

They know who I am, for goodness' sake. *They* called *me*.

They are telling me to open the front door wide, to let them in. I'm letting a complete stranger into the wide chasm of my life's history, all buried in the pixels of my technical device?

I am suspicious and confused.

Part of me is afraid my life is about to fade to black, and the other half is on high alert.

"Excuse me, can you please give me some identification as I have no idea who I am talking to?"

"Of course. My company ID number is 945DG34."

"Oh, OK, so what do you require me to do?"

"Go to the settings on your computer and type in your password and allow remote access to me."

"Um, I'm not quite sure what my password is."

"No problem, I'll wait on the line."

I walk up the stairs, sit down at my computer and freeze. My internet is as efficient as can be. I have no problems currently. Something feels fishy, actually even fishier than last week's "past-date-coded" barramundi.

I return to the intruder.

"Hello there, I am sorry. I will not be giving you my password. I will phone the internet head office and ascertain if I have a problem."

"There is a hacker on your computer right at this minute, obtaining all your details, so I would suggest you do exactly what I say right now."

"No, I will not—I have no idea who you are!"

An abusive stream of foul language attacks my middle ear.

"I will lose my job! I will lose my job! Give me your password! Give me your password!"

I drop the phone like a hot brick, block the number and then surf the local community social media page to ascertain whether anyone else has also been in the "scamming" line.

And they have.

Scams are becoming more persistent. We are working more at home. We are online more. Cyber criminals are very opportunistic. They are lurking in the cyber world, ready to pounce on "oldies" ineptitude.

My mum at the age of eighty called me delirious with excitement. She had received a letter from Nigeria informing her that she was the recipient of the first prize of millions in a lottery. Money was to be deposited into her account, which she was required to provide immediately or the prize would be lost. She couldn't remember her banking details, and while the caller waited patiently on the line as she ferreted through her paperwork, her neighbour walked in through her unlocked door to drop in a hot loaf of bread just purchased from the bakery.

My mum was exuberant in her excitement of recounting her winning story to said neighbour while fiddling through her multiple VIP notebooks. The neighbour placed her feet firmly back down on the ground. This scam had been doing the rounds. My mum hadn't been part of the information circle, and luckily this time a crisis was averted.

My friend loves to socialise with her BFFs, enjoying on occasion a tipple too much that drives her into early slumber in the backseat of the ride home.

She had had a really good night, celebrating in all the communal weekly accomplishments of the group. Slumber arrived a little earlier than advisable.

The driver followed instructions to her destination and woke her up on arrival with a shake and a shout. This was easy as on this occasion she had decided to sit in the front seat of the vehicle with her handbag casually flung to the side, which was now spilling its contents on arrival at her front door. The driver asked if she needed assistance to get out and get in. Cautious survival awareness locked in, and she confidently, yet sleepily, strode up the path and through her front door, alone and straight to bed.

All seemed just fine.

The evening was a success, but something was bothering her. She couldn't remember the journey home.

Friends from the night of celebration called her number to recount the evening's memories. Venus from Downtown Lays (names changed, of course) was enthusiastically answering and not their beloved friend. Money was cascading rapidly out of her accounts. No government department or banking body believed she was who she was. All documents had been hijacked, changed and disappeared, and now she, who was now identity-less, seemed to have disappeared too. She had no way of proving who she was.

This is nasty stuff.

Cyber criminals are becoming smarter in their evolving tactics and processes. We need to remain alert. They know we are older and less savvy in our tech skills.

Scammers can ascertain where you were born, your birth date, your mother's maiden name and much more if you spruik this all over your social media accounts (if you have them) or are careless with password notebooks or a big mouth.

If they claim your life identity, you will spiral into deep, dark nothingness, and it's so extremely hard to have the courage to climb back up.

Scammers want what you have. It has taken a lifetime for you to gather. Don't now throw it all away.

Watch out, and be alert for red flags. They are dangerous. They say STOP.

JUST A THOUGHT

"Curiosity pulls people into the scam."

– Frank Stallone

SENIOR SAGE

We need to stay smart and alert and aware. And, we don't need to be afraid to ask others if they have had the same experience. We don't need to feel foolish. We need to all stick together. We need to all learn together.

Fight and Forgive

STUFF HAPPENS IN FAMILIES.

Those from the same blood seem to blurt out in frustration and anger more readily than they do with a stranger.

Or, at the other end of the scale, they hide behind masks of deception, duping their DNA tribe with the perception that love and anger and jealousy are all pureed into one noncommittal, "all is good" emotion.

Nobody wants to feel like a loser. Nobody wants to confess to financial woes. Nobody wants to admit they are lonely. Nobody wants to fail—more so especially to their kin.

Frustration finds a home, and nothing is real.

Family occasions are fraught with danger with this subterfuge lurking and—BOOM!—the air becomes hot enough to fry an egg, and a flurry of angry words attack with force.

It escalates. There is rapid departure and lack of contact, and the new neighbour replaces family, this time more open and real.

Christmastime can be fraught with danger with different schedules and expectations and noise and clamour and confined spaces and lack of independence—oh boy—joyful or woeful. It's a little glimpse at what multigenerational families spend a whole year working out, all crammed into little space and constant togetherness.

Of course, these occasions are more rare at present, and communing is steering more toward chatting through the pixels. Tops are partying while bottoms remain in isolation holiday, wrapped in cosy pajamas or comfy well-worn trackies. Facebook and Instagram are the communication of the day. Now there are no more family rebukes or attacks when all are thrown together.

The online nastiness, however, can become far more cruel and ferocious.

Subtle exclusion causes perception of disfavour and ensuing anxiety, and notice is taken of all the liking and commenting and re-commenting and hearts and claps and waves. Doubt creeps in, and worries niggle about what was said, wasn't said, should have been said, forgot to be said in the fully fledged crisis of approval.

Fight or flight, comment or ignore, attack or retreat?

Attacking results in an insidious, manipulative online brawl. The relationship shuts down, and it's back to the neighbour to establish some friendly contact.

But really, is it worth it? Is this feud in the clan necessary? Is this the legacy we want to leave?

Let's give peace a try!

HOW ABOUT THIS AS AN ACTION PLAN:

1. Write out a list of all your family members.
2. Mark the family members who you haven't spoken to for a while.

3. Call or text or email each one of the family members, one a day, and tell them you are thinking of them.
4. Tell your family members you love them.
5. Call your children, however far away they are, and tell them you are always there.
6. Write a list of those to whom you have done wrong and are sorry.
7. Call or text or email these people, and say you are sorry.
8. Tell someone in a shop or takeout venue or service industry that they have done a wonderful job (if they have) and thank them.
9. Thank those who go unnoticed for the everyday, invisible jobs they do.
10. Commune with the homeless with two hot drinks and two masks and ask them their story. You may be the only one they talk to today.
11. Cuddle your dog or your bunny or your harmless pet snake (just joking). They are also family.
12. Volunteer and spread the love.
13. Be at peace if you get nothing back.

All in all, it will be a good day if you are taken unexpectedly tomorrow.

JUST A THOUGHT

“To us, family means putting your arms around each other and being there”

– Barbara Bush

SENIOR SAGE

If you walk through life with a scar on your heart, nobody else can feel the pain. Heal those scars and walk with love. You have everything to gain. Forgiving simply frees yourself from all burden.

R U OK?

FRIDAY NIGHT IS DATE NIGHT.

Six p.m. glass of wine, chocolate, pizza, movies—bliss!

This has been our tradition for decades, and I am pleased to say that our offspring also like this tradition and have continued to honour. They, too, are shutting off their work brains and immersing themselves in someone else's story, cuddled up comfortably in their suburban movie house.

This end-of-week reward is joyfully anticipated. But it has all gone belly up at present in this moment of coronavirus precaution. We are in the vulnerable statistic, so are warned to be vigilant in our out-of-home relaxation. It is not as comfortable as it used to be as our date night moves to our favourite couch.

Our TV is not smart, and neither are we. We are not fully trained in entertainment tech. We have no fancy add-ons, and even if we did, we are clueless about leads and ports and insertions.

It is a minefield of tangles.

We grab our phones, which we have hidden for a date-night detox, and scroll feverishly through instructions for date-night dummies.

And this is what we get:

> *ANT-IN: Two or more ports for NTSC analog and ATSC off-air signals. These ports work for ATSC only if you have a HDTV with a built-in HDTV (or ATSC) tuner.*

Did you understand that? What the hell does it all mean?

ANT-IN—yes, we do have a few ants in. A reminder to myself to be more vigilant in my cleaning endeavours.

NTSC—New Talent for Senior Citizens? Yes, this is fast becoming a new talent!

ATSC—All Together Senior Citizens. Yes, co-senior and I are in this together, but our rhetoric is becoming harsher.

Co-senior is on the floor because his knees don't bend properly, but he can't see where to input anything and is persevering with a poke at the indent of a neatly hidden screw.

I, in the meantime, am also on the floor with a side twist neck bend. I can see the input holes but can't see the matchy-matchy union.

I can't return my neck to its initial position, and my contorted joints are now stuck.

Our "reward for a busy week" night is now ruined. Co-senior and I are in full-force, accusation blame game.

The offering from "free-to-air channels" dates back to our youth. The replays may work as the content is lost somewhere in the memory bank. But it all feels so ho-hum and lacklustre.

We crave to be out, to talk, to laugh, to share in the company of friends and to freely explore our world once again, the world that has temporarily changed and shut down. This communal separation is tearing us apart, and we feel jagged at the edges.

Community and communication are paramount to complete our whole, especially more so as age slowly creeps up on us.

Our movie nights are not the same.

We feel alone and lonely.

We call people in other countries where dawn is breaking, sadly looking for comfort that they are feeling exactly the same way.

No one answers.

We text, "Hi, beautiful, how did your week go?"

No reply.

Are others having fun again on a Friday night?

Does anybody out there remember us?

Are we all so encased in this bubble of isolation that it is too burdensome to smash through the shell?

Our searches become more frenetic.

All we ask is validation that we are all sitting in exactly the same space at home, so it is OK.

We are blank.

We sit, we stare, we sink.

We have nothing.

We have reached the night of our soul. Is this a dark and sad and uncomfortable place for our friends too?

There is an "us" in this doldrum.

But what if there were just an "I"?

How are you feeling on a Friday night, alone, when the sun goes down and the sky drizzles its tears?

Was it you who rang when I was scrolling through my misery?

Was that your number that I didn't notice to answer?

Did you connect in your desolate recluse?

Are you drowning in alcohol and medication to push back pain and loneliness?

What does it feel like for the single and lonely out there?

Are they doing the same thing?

Are they reaching out for photo albums to recall the beauty of memories? Are these memories desperate in their recollection, wanting to be shared in their loneliness?

Do we hear the desperation?

Do we dismiss all this intrusion to be dealt with in the morning if we remember? Do *we* reach out and say "r u ok?"

Do we?

Do we?

Do it. Just do it!

Friday nights may have also been their date-and-reward night, which has now evolved into this cesspool of bleeding loneliness.

Souls can sometimes reach their rock bottom, and enough can become enough.

The shiny exterior we all seem to feel compelled to display is not the whole story.

People can ache unseen.

It is time now for you to see that ache—pick up that damn phone and say, "Hi, are you ok?"

Those four words could just save a life.

JUST A THOUGHT

"Place your hand over your heart. Can you feel it? That is called purpose. You're alive for a reason, so don't ever give up."

– *Unknown*

SENIOR SAGE

People are good at hiding where they are really at. They feel embarrassed to show their "real me." They feel like a failure, and they don't ask for help. Let's be little antennas, recognising this loneliness. Let's reach out and save some souls. Do not fear professional help if it all gets too much. (Listen to Matthew West: *Truth be Told*)

Prostrate for Prostate

HIBERNATION IS MAKING US LAZY IN OUR MEDICAL checks.

Before we know it, months have passed, and we can't now remember what needs to be checked and when.

(Just a little aside, people—download the free senior's Joy List at https://imnowcalledasenior.com/joylist to be on top of all checks and balances.)

Those with female bits are probably more consistent and reliable in making sure their body parts are healthy. But not so our menfolk, who need to be prodded gently into having their sensitive bits checked. I am sure for you, as it is for me, it is up to us to keep our eyes on the ball, make the call and book them in.

Co-senior, with much reluctance, fronts up to our regular GP. He hasn't had much checked for a while, boasting that he has never been fitter and puffing up his muscles to prove that he is still in muscle-retention mode.

He is ready for the ignominious prostate check. I can understand why he has been tardy. Our GP is old school and insists on the digit dance up the posterior.

Undressing rapidly and displaying high-jump competition-winner techniques, co-senior jumps on the bed mimicking our new poodle guarding a bone. All four limbs are attached to the bed, with head touching down and area of investigation reaching for the stars with a brown eye closely observing the approaching plastic glove.

At this point, so said GP lowers his glasses, misty with mirth, and through staccato guffaws, advises that prostates are not checked in this position but delicately tucked up in foetal mode. Co-senior hasn't had a check for a while, so we can excuse his error.

Co-senior is rather pleased, as his knees have taken a beating in the entry to seniorhood and are battling to stand firm. He rolls over onto his side, hiding his embarrassment and blesses the fact that this GP had seen all his body parts over the years as well as other patient's anatomies, so nothing is likely to shock.

A little advice from co-senior. Check your spelling before your next checkup. The word is *prostate*, not *prostrate*. The extra *R* is not required for your next annual medical check.

JUST A THOUGHT

It is very frightening when you're told you have any form of the C-word, but because of early detection, they caught it before it had hardly begun. I'm completely cured and will go on to have a wonderful, fruitful life. I'll never die of prostate cancer.

– Mandy Patinkin

SENIOR SAGE

Health issues happen when one gets older, so the importance of being vigilant even in difficult times is paramount.

Slow Down

THE WORLD HAD GONE DARK.
The world has shut down.
When I open my window, there's nothing I see, and it's calm.

The world is at war,
Our lungs needing more.
When I read all the news, I look up and I pray and implore.

Is it time to slow down and reset?
Is it time now to think and reconnect?

Oh, slow down, slow down.
Once again, we see blue in the sky.
Oh, slow down, slow down,
The buildings are cleaner as they rise.
Oh, slow down, slow down,
I can see your face again,
And this world is once again all yours and mine.

Do we want what we had?
Was some of it bad?

Will we learn from the past and rather be glad?
Can we now make a change?
Learn how to rearrange?
Will the future be beautiful in the new way of our days?

Oh, slow down, slow down,
Once again, we see blue in the sky.
Oh, slow down, slow down,
The buildings are cleaner as they rise.
Oh, slow down, slow down,
I can see your face again,
And this world is once again all yours and mine.

Written and performed by Julie

JUST A THOUGHT

"Slow down, and enjoy the journey right now. Take time for the people in your life. They won't always be there."

– Joel Osteen

SENIOR SAGE

Why do we rush around all the time? Take time to breathe, and work out what really is important. It will serve your soul well in the long run.

Writer's Block

TODAY WAS THE DAY—THE DAY FOR PROLIFIC WRITING, succinct comments and intellectual commentary.

My computer beckoned. My morning routine waited. I plonked myself in front of the screen, took a deep breath, fingers itching for action, and *nothing*.

Are you an author?

Is there sometimes…*nothing*?

I was dreaming all night about life-changing content. This morning, there is *nothing*.

Herein lies the problem.

I have mislaid my idea notebook that sleeps on the side table next to my bed. We work in tandem during the night, but I think it is playing hide-and-seek between the ruffled sheets. We usually have a harmonious rhythm—sleep, wake, thought bubble, scribble, sleep. And again and again. No wonder I have *nothing* this morning.

My bedside light is playing tag with the notebook, as its also treasuring its hiding place. The main bedroom light has relocated. I blame a little home decoration renovation that has lately been utilising my time. The bed has found a new position, and spacial awareness in the middle of the black of night hasn't caught up. I discover this quite dramatically when my forehead connects with an unusually situated wall.

Maybe my brain is in recovery this morning, and any further input or output will not be helpful in recovery, so it's in rest mode.

I have

nothing.

But nothing is good!!!

It is the first rung of the ladder of *meditation.*

Maybe this is where I am meant to be this morning. submitting to the beauty of nothingness.

I decide to go where my nothing brain is leading me.

I am inspired and motivated by *nothingness.*

> *Be still and know yourself as the Truth you have been searching for. Be still and let the inherent joy of that Truth capture your drama and destroy it in the bliss of consummation. Be still and let your life be lived by the purpose you were made for. Be still and receive the inherent truth of your heart. (Gangaji)*

1. I find a quiet spot (could have been in front of the computer as there is absolutely nothing going on in here—my brain is very quiet). Sometimes the floor is the best spot if I can get up again.
2. I close my eyes.
3. I *breathe.*
4. I focus on my breath and the movement of my body while breathing.

5. I breathe in through my nose and breathe out through my mouth. (Some people breathe out through their nose.)
6. I breathe in blue and breathe out red (no mixed colour palettes here. I don't breathe in red; it makes me anxious.)
7. My spirit settles.
8. My mind is empty.
9. Ahhhh, I remember what I should be writing.
10. Not now—the thought disappears like a floating cloud.
11. I notice my breathing.
12. I am aware of my breathing.
13. Ommmmmm. Ommmmmmm. Ommmmmm.
14. I'm asleep.

I am less stressed and anxious. Nothingness makes me calm. I feel kind. I feel centred.

Psychologist Dr Carl Stonier, from the University of Hull, published an incredible study in the academic compilation "Potentiating Health and the Crisis of the Immune Study":

> One shining example of Dr. Stonier's study was a woman deemed the "*cardiac cripple.*" With her medication maxed out and incapable of another bypass surgery, she was out of options and *out of hope*.
>
> Luckily, the guided meditation proved to be *her magic*. The same woman who got an-

> gina from simply getting out of her car was, after practicing meditation for only three months, swimming nearly a mile every day.
>
> While nothing in the past had worked for her, she ended up maintaining *good health for decades* afterward, even becoming the caregiver to her husband who developed Alzheimer's later in life.[2]

So there you go—meditation is so very good for you. I found it unexpectedly.

Search for your expert—your Zen master.

I am a beginner, an enthusiastic beginner. But, by gosh, I spring up off the floor, fly back to my computer and remember what I wanted to talk about in this chapter.

It was meditation.

It took ten minutes of self-awareness, peace, breathing and mind-stress dump for my subliminal sleepy thoughts to resurface and share exactly what I was meant to share with you today.

JUST A THOUGHT

"To a mind that is still, the whole universe surrenders."

– *Anonymous*

SENIOR SAGE

You will never know the peace and calm in "nothingness" unless you give it a try.

How to Find Your Purpose

YEAH YEAH, ALL HAIL TO THE MOTIVATIONAL GURUS chanting "Woop, woop, find your purpose. You will be free. It will change your life."

It all seems to be so gloriously spectacular as they run off to slide down their purposeful rainbow, only communicating in happy high fives and ear-to-ear grins. They are fully programmed into their why. They are swimming in an ocean of joy and meaning.

Not you? I gathered so.

Is there a meandering river of unidentified purpose running through your veins?

Do you feel bored and boring because the days are just happening and re-happening and re-happening?

Do you feel unimaginative and passionless? Which way do you go? How do you even start to work it all out?

We revisit the past to find some inspiration. We are trying so hard to dig deep and find a connection with what used to be. But it simply does not blow our hair back anymore.

We ask ourselves why.

Well, of course we have grown up, haven't we? We have experienced life in so many ways, and our eyes have been opened to so many more opportunities and interests—and guess what—we can do them. Of course, I'm not suggesting that jumping out of planes and deep-sea diving will become our favourite pastime, but who cares. We have evolved, we have grown, we have changed and we have aged, and it is all A-OK.

We are exactly where we are meant to be.

So....

We then try to commit to purpose, but we are uncommitted.

We don't have the urge anymore to follow through. We stop.

We sink back into boredom and our comfy couch.

Malaise settles back in.

And the cycle continues...

I hear you. It isn't fun—or funny?

So, it's time to make a plan, dear seniors.

Let's work it all out so we can find our vooma again.

Let's think through a mighty good plan to get us right back on track.

Let's become enthusiastic little bunnies once again.

Let's feel alive again.

Let's shock our family and friends into saying, "I want what she is having!"

Let's get back into life once again.

Identifying the passion is sometimes not easy. We first need to recognise that we *want* to break out of this cocoon of isolation and retirement and non-relevance. Once we recognise that, we can do better. We give ourselves permission to live our best life.

This is the first rung of the ladder.

I have been there. I understand.

So here is what works for me and could very well work for you:

- Find a pen and paper.
- Be still, be very still.
- Be alone, close your eyes and breathe.
- Clear your mind from the grocery list and the unfolded laundry and the ache in your knee.
- Be still, breathe in and out.

LIST ONE

Write it down, and don't skip this step:

- What comes easy to you?
- What do you naturally do well?
- What makes you feel—really feel, right down inside feel, lighting-a-spark-that-would-illuminate-the-sky feel?
- What do others do that make you feel unsettled and frustrated that you are not doing the same and are being left behind?
- What makes your pulse race and heart beat faster and makes you want to dance?
- What makes you curious?
- What do you love?

Now blend it all together.

What do you really love to do that you find easy to do, that comes naturally to you and for which you have a deep passion?

You don't need to bake the whole cake. You can add the ingredients, one by one.

There you go. First step done.

Are the couch sessions becoming less frequent?

Is there more of a spring in your step?

Maybe, just maybe, can you do it?

Congratulations.

But, oops, a little speed bump. We are expecting this.

At this point, you are probably telling yourself you are not able to achieve these things.

Your dark side is telling you that you are too old or don't have the knowledge or don't know where to start or don't have the brain capacity. Friends' suggestions and interference and societal perception start influencing you that the only appropriate action for a satisfied final quarter is bridge, gardening, golf and knitting. Gosh, I know that these hobbies can bring the spring back into the step for many, but are you sure? Can you push the boundaries just a little further?

Come on seniors, dig deep. If you really, truly love to participate in these, you have found your why. If not, crush these thoughts, stomp on them hard, scream at them and give them the flick.

OK, ready to continue?

List one (tick).

LIST TWO

- What are your most positive qualities?
- How can you use these positive qualities in achieving everything on list one?

List two (tick)

LIST THREE

Time to make it happen.

- Clarify your vision; clarify your why.
    - Write down three of your most fave things to do. (No more than three for now.)
- Create a vision board and visualise.
    - Write affirmations. Repeat these affirmations daily. You will be amazed at what you attract. Totally believe in yourself and your ability to be or do the above.
- Be very clear about what the choices are.
    - Take responsibility for your choices.
- Shine so strong that you attract the right people to help you make these life choices happen.
- Set SMART goals: **S**pecific, **M**easurable, **A**ttainable, **R**elevant, **T**ime-bound goals.

Yes, we are *smart*.

- Your goals only matter to you and not anyone else.
- Find this passion—make it your purpose, and live your very best life.
- Fall in love with your purpose to align with your true and authentic destiny.

Three huge no-nos..

NO NEGATIVITY
NO NEGATIVE PEOPLE
NO NEGATIVE ENERGY.

There you go. You are on your way. Pen and paper out—go and buy yourself a beautiful notebook. It's back to school.

Time for some homework.

You can do it.

JUST A THOUGHT

"Chase your passion, not your pension."

– *Denis Waitley*

SENIOR SAGE

If you find your passion, you will find your purpose, and you will wake up each day with sunshine in your heart and light-filled days to follow.

Transformers

MY GRANDSON IS HAVING A *TRANSFORMERS* BIRTHDAY party.

I am an expert on *Paw Patrol* and Bluey and have now graduated to Transformers -as you know.

We are completely in sync with this new phase. I have secretly been watching YouTube videos to bring me up to speed.

My grandson thinks I am an awesome Gagga. We speak the same language.

I converse in Optimus Prime and Bumblebee.

"Look, Gagga," he screeches in delight as his little fingers Houdini his robot figure into a truck and then back again.

"Oh, my goodness, you are so clever!" I say the right thing. "Will you teach Gagga?"

I become student, and he becomes master, and I progress to a master class of Transformer transforming.

"Gagga, I am going to have a Transformers birthday party. You know I am turning four?" as he throws four fingers in the air.

We add it to our Google calendar.

While spiralling the zucchini tonight, with the whirr of the machine in close proximity to co-senior's ear, I advise him that it was soon to be party time again.

I advise him that it is a Transformers party.

Co-senior blinks wide-eyed. He looks startled.

I think he has been so engrossed in his TED Talks subscription that maybe he doesn't know too much about Transformers. He would certainly think a Transformer was connected to electrical supply.

I let it pass. He hasn't been in on our one-on-one nightly conversations, so he is missing vital information on Transformer education, so ably explained by our four-year- old grandson.

I remind co-senior that we are due to be in "*party-land* "the next day.

He is rustling down deep in my wardrobe. I think he is merely colour-coding my outfits as he likes precision, so I think nothing of planting a big kiss on his cheek and a thank you that he has found my boot that has been missing for months.

"It's going to be fun, sweetheart," I say.

"Are you ready? Let's go."

I climb into the car, turn on the engine, check my lipstick and adjust my side mirror, catching a glimpse of co-senior, manicured, coiffed, wigged and robed in my silk, plunging-V-neck dress accessorised with my red heels and matching red handbag.

Co-senior jumps into the car. "Do you like the look?" he asks.

I can't reply. I see another Mrs Doubtfire moment, this one more refined.

"Um, what exactly is going on?" I ask.

"What do you mean?" retorts co-senior. I could see he was hurt.

"I love your dress. It's so smooth and silky, and I think pink is my colour," he says with a wink.

I'm silently miffed that co-senior looks better in my dress than I do and subconsciously make a note to sign up to Weight Watchers.

But I am also adamant that the time has now come for co-senior's appointment at the audiology centre for his hearing check.

If a Transformers party has meta-morphed into a *trans-gender* party, the "duck" party that is our next invitation could become a very big problem.

JUST A THOUGHT

"Today you are You, that is truer than true. There is no one alive who is Youer than You."

– *Dr Seuss*

SENIOR SAGE

It doesn't matter who anyone is. So long as they are their true, authentic self, then that is all that matters.

The Ponytail

HAIRDRESSING SALONS SEEM TO BE SAFE—AND THEN not safe.

Co-senior is morphing, as a result, into a cross between David Beckham, Karl Lagerfeld and Johnny Depp, introducing a further degree of individuality—a shiny pate with hair growth in more abundance around the lower portion of the anatomical head.

I remind co-senior that I purchased a very sharp pair of scissors when I thought I may try some clothes' alteration sewing techniques in my isolation state. I also assure him that I have been following a do-it-yourself learn-a-new-skill video, and I am coming up trumps. I am absolutely sure I can snip and tidy very well, including the addition of a few on-trend layers or two.

I did have a mini practice on my own hair. It wasn't exactly a perfect success, but hey, who is looking? We aren't allowed out anyway, and by the time we have some form of normalcy, the one side will have caught up with the other.

I encourage co-senior to become emancipated, tie his curls up in a large scrunchy and exhibit his inner femininity. Then again, who said anything about feminine. On our visit to Jerusalem, this look was perfectly normal in some religious quarters and is, in fact, an absolute mark of honour, prestige and learned sophistication.

I even suggested we could go artsy-fartsy and put colours and patterns in the ties, and he could borrow one of my earrings if he wanted to complete the look. Conservative co-senior was not loving the idea—he felt the ponytail wasn't quite his look, and he wanted to maintain his very own form of conservative individuality.

I managed to get one week of the long hair.

I then continued my suggestions that he should also have a no-shave day, sporting a Neanderthal look just for a fleeting moment.

I then noticed that he was styling his own take on freedom and was rather enjoying it. Together with resting his skin, he had donned a thobe he had purchased on our Petra adventure, and freedom was now taking on a full-body experience.

Our physical bodies had a momentary glimpse of freedom until Mama Senior morphed into Mama "Scissorhands" to work on cleaning up her ponytailed, freedom-loving, grey-haired, co-senior fuzzball.

The famous final expose was rather unusual, but I am a good student and ready to improve. Who knows—this could become a successful new suburban home industry, if it's something that floats my boat.

What have you learned in isolation?

Are you excited about a fledgling new skill?

JUST A THOUGHT

"And then humidity said, 'Today I'll make you look like the *Lion King*.'"

– *Hotmessmoms*

SENIOR SAGE

There is freedom in letting natural colour show its face and natural style embrace the face.

The Cloud

I LOVE MY OFFICE AS AT LAST WE HAVE HAD A GARDEN haircut and I can see out of my window.

Yes, little kangaroo, I did see you jumping across the driveway.

Kookookookookaka

I hear you, kookaburra, defending your position on the telephone wire.

I can see the sky today, and it makes me smile. The rain has drenched for the past month, and now it is sunny and clear. As the sun sets in front of me, a prepossessing pink and blue and white cloud floats across my view, glorious in its variegation, and I feel good. It looks so soft and warm and inviting.

My mind wanders back to the window seat of my last flight, floating through the misty ruffles of untouchable white magic, mysterious and replete in nothingness.

The clouds I see look like cotton wool.

So what, then, is this "cloud" everyone talks about that is going to safely store all my documents and writing?

How is it going to keep my life safe, and where do I find it all if everyone's stuff is all in the same cloud? How does it remain separate?

I don't want my life to blend in with my community groups. I don't want to know their business. I want to remain an individual.

I am happy and confident that our memorabilia boxes are safely resting in storage. They are beautifully labelled and ready at any point for rapid extraction. And now I have to trust something called "the cloud" with a new definition. This definition is not in our vocabulary.

"Sweethearts, where exactly is this cloud?" we ask our children.

"Is it intangible phwoah, or is there a massive cloud situated somewhere that is sucking in and storing all this information?

Is this just abstract newspeak and (sigh) something else we need to learn?"

Our children raise their eyebrows, ready to settle into a tech-storage lecture. We are not really interested. What has worked for us still works for us, and now we have to convert our whole depository warehouse into an abstract theme.

The only cloud we can see is in the sky, so who exactly is storing this?

Is God up there holding on to all our data? He has it all under control anyway. He knows about it all anyway, so why do we need to even bother loading him up with more stuff?

He has his own filing system; it will just make him confused.

(Eeek! We are now meant to be politically correct, so if we are made in God's image, maybe he is a she because I am a she. I am getting even more confused.)

Our children inform us that this data is stored on several different servers in a number of different locations. I presume that some of this data is in Spain and the rest in India or maybe hovering in satellite servers somewhere in the sky. Heaven forbid if we need to hastily locate a document. Who owns this cloud—the universe? What happens if it rains—will we be drenched by everyone else's information as well as our own?

Is it like the "tip" where it all gets mulched in together and jangled birth records give some of us an extra number of years?

On our very last cruise, taken thankfully before ships were forced into early retirement, I met the friend I was meant to meet. She had left her iPad on a tour bus and was well assured that all her data would be expediently re-downloaded to a new iPad from the cloud. We were now countries away from the lost iPad, but she was safe and sound in the cloud or on the cloud or through the cloud. We were never quite that sure.

Oh well, we said to each other, we are good little seniors, and we are willing to learn. And if we are to survive, we need to stop looking out of the cruise ship window marvelling at the floating artworks in the sky with a cocktail in our hands. There is now much more to the cloud than there used to be. It is now a new landscape, and if we don't adapt, we die. So says Lt. Gen. Rick Lynch.

JUST A THOUGHT

Clouds (plural) are fluffy and ethereal and magical and penetrable. The Cloud(singular) stores data on the internet. I really don't know clouds at all.

– Julie

SENIOR SAGE

Some people are happy in their old world. Some people are happy in the new. There is no need to be restless; just be happy in your own world.

All Night Long

Bedtime
Brush teeth
Take tablets
Wash splint
Spread creams
Turn on air conditioner
Sip chamomile tea
Peck co-senior
Nightie-night to Facebook
Nightie-night to Instagram
Turn on sports programme
Drone

Black

Wake to drone
Switch off drone

Black

Wake to bladder
Eyes closed
Bathroom shuffle
Relief
Bed

Black

Dream of not finding a toilet
Wake to bladder
Eyes closed
Bathroom shuffle
Relief
Co-senior turns
Bed

Black

Wake to neighbours
Turn on phone
5.15 a.m.
Eyes open
Bathroom shuffle
Relief
Co-senior snoring
Bed

Worry about health
Worry about bills
Worry about family
Worry about deadlines
Worry about washing hanging out in the rain
Worry about emails
Worry about weight
Worry about bladder
Worry about coronavirus

Bathroom shuffle
No relief
Bed
No sleep

Promise to myself to go to bed earlier
Promise to myself no bluelight before bed
Promise to myself to try valerian or Rescue Remedy or melatonin or anything.

Morning
Wakey wakey for the day
Nudge co-senior
COFFEEEEEEE

Is this just me, or is it also you?

Falcons Fly and Chickens Can't

CO-SENIOR IS MUMBLING AND GRUMBLING THIS morning.

His knees are sore, and he is not hearing well.

Mixed in with all this is a cavalcade of yawns and squeaks as he walks up and down stairs, balancing what is needed upstairs and what is needed downstairs.

I was nasty. I told him he was acting old.

I told him he had eaten too much sugar.

I told him it was lack of sleep and vit D, and he should be taking better care of himself.

A fleeting shadow crossed his face. I had touched a sensitive nerve.

Co-senior withdraws.

I walk on eggshells.

I try to justify his aging by saying, "Hey, you are over seventy, you know, so you are allowed to act old! Mum and Dad were really old at that age!"

No response.

I change tack.

"You know, I have just read about a ninety-fiver riding to golf twice a week and hitting a mean ball. Why don't you go and hit some balls?"

Nothing.

"Stop feeling sorry for yourself. Barbara Peters was eighty-one and still putting younger ballet dancers to shame! And look, here is another eighty-year-old twirling up and down a pole. Should we try that?"

Co-senior does not respond.

Then I start on positive reinforcement.

"You know, you need to think young, behave young, walk young—be young. The mind is a powerful thing. Work on it. You will attract what you want to become. If you say you can, you can; if you say you can't, you can't.

You know Beethoven was deaf and created masterpieces!"

Now I am starting to irritate myself.

He looks blank.

Then I start to worry.

Is co-senior really getting old?

Am I fighting so hard to keep him young so I can do life with him for many more decades?

Falcons dive at four hundred miles per hour. They are powerful flyers with big flight muscles. They are made this way.

Chickens don't have the same power or wings. They are not made to fly. But they powerfully lay eggs that nutritionally work for us.

A falcon is not a chicken and vice versa. They are different.

In the same way, a seventy-two-year-old is not a twenty-five-year-old. They are different.

It is time for me to see and understand this and coax co-senior to hear all the future promises whispering to his soul.

Co-senior has had some solid extra sleep, some good aerobic exercise, gallons of water, some blueberries, vitamins B and C, probiotics and some good healthy fibre-rich carbs.

Co-senior is back on the train of life. He is his sparkly former self.

He is beginning to look like Brad Pitt.

It's time for my eye check appointment.

I am now the one who feels old.

Co-senior is at the pool for his morning exercise. He has left his phone at home. I run to his study to answer.

"Oh, hello, this is Scarlet from Pole Dancing Academy. Just calling to confirm that classes for your husband commence next week. Could you let him know? Thank you."

I freeze.

Damn, I have pushed co-senior out of the nest. My aging chicken has now become a strong, powerful falcon.

And falcons are hunting birds too….Just bring back my clucking chicken.

This hen will peck no more.

JUST A THOUGHT

"Be motivated like the falcon; hunt gloriously. Be magnificent as the leopard; fight to win. Spend less time with nightingales and peacocks. One is all talk, the other only colour."

– *Rumi*

SENIOR SAGE

We will all grow older, but if we take care of ourselves, our minds will not reflect our bodies; our minds will soar like falcons.

Is It the Devil or God?

We are in a mess! Or have we suddenly and unexpectedly and temporarily been liberated from the whirlwind of life?

This is where we stand…

Millions of people are sick—really sick—all around the world. Thousands of people are dying.

Some are vigilantly wearing masks, and some are vigilantly reviling those who do and those who don't.

We are all suspicious of human touch. We struggle when forced to isolate. It is not natural for the human spirit.

Despite all this, do we really want to go back to the world we once knew, or are we making plans to work out how to thrive in a new world order?

Is this good or bad?

Here is the good:

We are communicating more in families.

We eat together at communal tables.

We are listening and sharing and embracing the simple.

We see the sky again, and our monuments stand out in their unpolluted form.

There is a place for all of us on our roads.

We are learning that standing together and loving globally will fix us all.

New recipes are being explored, and new courses discovered.

New songs and poems and books are being written and new words created.

Technology is not the enemy.

We communicate freely with friends and family without anxiety.

Special occasions are still special despite being in another form.

We are kinder and more helpful and more loving.

We are breathing.

God knows about all of this—he is right in the mix, I believe. Did our Supreme Being, for those who believe, decide to take drastic measures?

Is it time to reflect on the fragility of life and understand the importance of each minute?

Is it time to understand it is out of our control?

Is it time to be grateful?

Is it time to be spiritually challenged?

Is it time for us to love all humans?

Is it time for less complacency?

Is it time to challenge ourselves to be the very best we possibly can be and when we reach that best to aspire to the next rung of the ladder?

We now have a bit more time to think, do we not, so how about we start thinking?

There is also a reverse, however…

There are violent members lurking in some homes. Where does one run and hide without retribution?

The pantry screams out to us to indulge in heart-clogging ingredients, and we cannot resist. Our insulin levels are soaring from sugar consumption. Our arteries are closing from cholesterol and trans fats. Diseases are grabbing hold in our resistance to GP checks.

We can be lonely and sad.

Mental health is now at the forefront of our vocabulary.

Has God had enough, or has the devil been in charge?

Is it the light, or is it the dark that hold the reins (if you believe in these forces)?

Are we shaking and shifting to something better?

Who knows?

The surrounding noise has, however, stilled, and we can breathe again. And, in this virginal space, we find there is more to earthly life. We are spiritually challenged and are bonded together in crisis. We are grateful for life.

We are all the ingredients in this large earthly pie. Life will taste so much better when these ingredients are organically sourced from compassion, patience, unselfishness, positivity, joy and of course love.

We are all in this together, so let's make our next taste of life the best meal we have ever had.

JUST A THOUGHT

"You, me, or nobody is gonna hit as hard as life. But it ain't about how hard you hit. It's about how hard you can get hit and keep moving forward."

– Sylvester Stallone

SENIOR SAGE

Take this time, seniors, to reinvent yourselves. Learn a new skill, go through your photo albums and get them into order, prepare new recipes, let your hair run wild. Let your mind influence your day, not the media or environment.

The List

ALL HAIL TO THE LIST MAKERS, MY SOUL SISTERS.
I need a list.
I can't exist without the list.
I struggle to detox on holiday without a list.
I am delirious with glee when I can tackle my list again.
I need to know when to pay accounts.
I need to know everyone's birthdays. I am good at this.
I need to show up for an appointment.
It is all on a list.

However,
I am stressed.
The list never ends.
I transfer and add to tomorrow's list.
I am exhausted.
I am a prolific, proficient list builder, and here is what I have learned.

STEP ONE: SET UP

- Buy a bright notebook or planner that distinctly screams GOALS! Make it unique, unusual and obvious.
- Buy a correction pen or correction tape.
- Set your goals at the beginning of the year.
- Section these goals under different headings:
    - Spiritual
    - Health
    - Family
    - Friends
    - Development
    - Purchases
    - House
    - Income providing
    - Volunteering and philanthropy
    - To learn
    - To read
    - To watch
    - Fun
    - Books to write (that is just mine)
    - Holiday destinations to visit

Then you add on your very own headings.

STEP TWO: ESTABLISHING YOUR GOALS

Monthly goals

Write out your *monthly goals* taken from this list—just one month, the month you are in. Anything more than that scrambles your brain

Weekly goals

It's time to break down again. Write your *weekly goals* taken from your monthly goals.

What's your focus for this week—just this week, not next week and the week after?

Daily goals

Finally, what are you going to do *today* to make this happen?

Identify just *one thing* that will make everything else easier.

Read all about it here: *The One Thing* by Gary Keller and Jay Papasan

Then do it.

STEP THREE: TACKLE YOUR LIST

- Attack the list with gusto, preferably in the morning when your brain is alive.
- Tackle your list in blocks of time.
- Avoid doing all the easy items first. Tackle the tricky, icky, ugly, procrastination to-dos first. Fun comes later.

- Avoid a high-carb lunch, which doesn't auger well for a productive afternoon.
- Tackle the easier jobs after lunch.
- Remember to take breaks.
- Accomplish your *one thing*. It will make your list shorter tomorrow.

STEP FOUR: TIGHTEN YOUR LIST

Be sure to include these on your list:

- Exercise
- Healthy eating
- Stretches
- Antioxidants
- Laughs
- Gratitude
- Water
- Breathing
- Meditation

You may be stretched, but you won't be stressed. Use your corrector to expunge and obliterate.

Do you notice more and more white space on the page? It's *so* good for your stress levels.

What is your goal?

1. A blank piece of paper.
2. Nothing.
3. Sleep—dreaming of blank pages.

Keep your list updated. Keep a notebook next to your bed, just in case. Sift regularly through the monthly to-dos. Some are superfluous, so discard those that do not fuel the dream.

Those dreams simply weren't the right dreams for you.

JUST A THOUGHT

"Love them or hate them, informational posts presented in list format are easily digestible, and allow for an efficient transfer of your value proposition to the reader."

– Brian Clark, founder, Copyblogger
(Now this sounds very hoity-toity, does it not?)

SENIOR SAGE

Some people really don't like making lists and each to their own. They seem to still function in their free spirited way. Maybe they are Google calendar experts, or make notes on their devices and it works for them .Somehow as a senior,a good old notebook and spreadsheet does the trick if you can only work out how to create one.

Tech Terror

I KNOW, YOU KNOW, WE ALL KNOW THAT THIS IS HOW it goes.

I know, you know, we all know that it has happened to us.

I know, you know, we all know….

"Where is a human we can talk to?"

SENIOR TRYING TO RESET PASSWORD

WINDOWS:	Please enter your new password
USER:	cabbage
WINDOWS:	Sorry, the password must be more than 8 characters
USER:	boiled cabbage
WINDOWS:	Sorry, the password must contain 1 numerical character
USER:	1 boiled cabbage
WINDOWS:	Sorry, the password cannot have blank spaces
USER:	50damnboiledcabbages

WINDOWS:	Sorry, the password must contain at least one uppercase character
USER:	50DAMNboiledcabbages
WINDOWS:	Sorry, the password cannot use more than one uppercase character consecutively
USER:	50damnBoiledCabbagesS-hovedUpYourAssIfYouDon'tGiveMeAc-cessNow!
WINDOWS:	Sorry the password cannot contain punctuation.
USER:	ReallyPissedOff50DamnBoiledCabbag-esShovedUpYourAssIfYouDontGiveMe-AccessNow
WINDOWS:	Sorry, that password is already in use

This scenario is on a Facebook page and a Laughing Matter page and another page and another page, and… So it is out there. It wouldn't be out there in such volume if it weren't happening to most of us, now would it?

JUST A THOUGHT

“Never trust anything that can think for itself if you can’t see where it keeps its brain.”

– J.K. Rowling, author of the Harry Potter books

SENIOR SAGE

Sometimes when we are shaking, we are being forced to change and grow. We are simply shifting to something better.

Coronavirus Replaces Terrorism

"HON, COME HERE QUICKLY," CO-SENIOR SHOUTS from the bedroom.

I am immersed in magnesium salts, luxuriating in my pre-beddy-byes bath.

"Quickly!"

It sounds urgent. Is this a medical emergency? Has he stepped on the needle I lost when sewing on a button this morning? Has a funnel-web spider found a home in his shoe?

I jump out of the bath and drip through to the bedroom.

Co-senior is sitting upright in front of the television set and points to the screen. He is speechless and alarmed.

I look over at the screen, wondering what could be so important, and watch the deadliest attack on US soil since the Pearl Harbor bombing that launched the United States into World War II.

My first reaction is that we are watching a terrible accident. But when the second aircraft hits, I know it is for real, and the seeds of fear have been planted. Our safety and security are violated, and we now need to develop subconscious protection armour and observant exteriors.

Everything for a while stands still.

We call our friends in the USA to see if they are OK. We call our families in different countries and states to see if they are OK. We are numb.

We become hypervigilant about delivered parcels or out-of-place street odours for fear of biological or nuclear weapons. We develop a fight-or-flight plan should we be in the middle of an attack.

Co-senior and I have never been part of an ANZAC Day celebration in Australia. This is the day that Australia commemorates all those who lost their lives in service to their country. This ANZAC tradition was established on 25 April, 1915, when the Australian and New Zealand Army Corps landed on the Gallipoli Peninsula. There are services and marches in cities and towns throughout the world where servicemen, servicewomen and peacemakers are stationed.

We book ourselves into a city hotel in Sydney and set our alarms for an early morning start. It feels thrilling and patriotic. We feel Australian. We feel like we belong.

Dressed in our warm anoraks and runners, we congregate at the Sydney Cenotaph for the Dawn Service.

> The Dawn Service observed on Anzac Day has its origins in an operational routine which is still observed by the Australian Army today. The half-light of dawn plays tricks with soldiers' eyes and from the earliest times the half-hour or so before dawn, with all its grey, misty shadows, became one

of the most favoured times for an attack. Soldiers in defensive positions were therefore woken up in the dark before dawn, so that by the time the first dull grey light crept across the battlefield they were awake, alert, and manning their weapons; This was, and still is, known as "Stand-to." It was also repeated at sunset.

After the First World War, returned soldiers sought the comradeship they felt in those quiet, peaceful moments before dawn. With symbolic links to the dawn landing at Gallipoli, a dawn stand-to or dawn ceremony became a common form of Anzac Day remembrance during the 1920s; the first official Dawn Service was held at the Sydney Cenotaph in 1927. Dawn services were originally very simple and followed the operational ritual; in many cases they were restricted to veterans only. The daytime ceremony was for families and other well-wishers, the Dawn Service was for old soldiers to remember and reflect among the comrades with whom they shared a special bond. Before dawn the gathered veterans would be ordered to "stand to" and two minutes of silence would follow. At the end of this time a lone bugler would play the "Last Post" and then concluded the service with "Reveille".[3]

We feel unbelievably honoured that this remembrance dawn service has opened for families and everyone who honours those who sacrificed for our future.

There are many people already in place when we arrive. Babies sleep soundly, tucked up in warm blankets. Little ones cling onto their handheld torchlights, swaying them from left to right, echoing the stars still illuminating the early morning sky. The place feels magical in the ethereal threads that are binding us humans, us Australians together.

Bang!

We all freeze.

Law enforcement is on the alert and rushes to investigate. The moment of connected, supportive unity is scattered. We are ready to run.

And then from around the corner….

"I'm knackered. Besh nite of ma life".

Hoots of laughter. The sound of keys slamming against barricades.

"What's the f@%#king time? Is there a party going on here? Mush be one 'ellever party with so many people."

Clunk.

The cops have it under control, and we can breathe again.

But we are alert.

We notice the barricades all around us preventing a purposeful vehicle. We notice law enforcement blending between families. We absorb the haunting "Last Post", but our eyes are wandering.

Such beauty in commemoration, such fear in anticipation.

And now, this appears to have been superseded by something even more dangerous. Before we were alert with our eyes. Now we can't see the attacker. It could be you or you or you or you. We don't know. We can't touch you, we can't sing with you, we can't stand right next to you, we can't hold each other's hands as connected brothers-in-arms. We are fearful and suspicious of you. We comment about your selfishness when not masked up or when you cough or sneeze with no protection. You comment on the fragility of our age and our vigilance in observing the rules for our protection.

We are always on high alert.

This is now terrorising us, and as I write, we are still in the middle of it all.

The car barricades now don't appear to be so prevalent, but the human barricades are.

We pray that all these forms of attack cease. We have law enforcement officers who create a wall between terror and us, and brilliant scientists who are now building a wall to fight this infection.

We optimistically stand together once again as brothers-in-arms and offer to help in any way to lay the bricks and build the defences. We need this barricade; we need it urgently.

This is a new form of terrorism, and we are all recruited to take our part in keeping the world free and safe and alive.

JUST A THOUGHT

"Terrorism has become the systematic weapon of a war that knows no borders or seldom has a face."

– Jacques Chirac

SENIOR SAGE

Let's work hard at nonviolence, kindness, peace, compassion, humility, and peaceful, healthy coexistence. We can do it. I know we can do it.

Give Creativity and Self-Help a Go

"I'M TOO OLD TO DO THAT!"

Really? Who is telling you that you are too old to do that?

Too *old* in that the expectations of yourself are limited because your age has increased?

Too *old* because your body and brain are tired and have capitulated to this thing called life?

Too *old* because other outer influencers don't see you as being capable?

Too *old* because you are scared of what others think of you if you fail?

It is all simply a state of mind. We can change that. For goodness' sake, a seventy-eight-year-old has been elected as the president of the United States. Who told him he was too *old*?

Atchley's Ohio Longitudinal Study of Aging and Retirement found that "people with more positive views of their own aging lived, on average, 7.6 years longer than people with negative views."[4]

Our bodies are perfectly in cahoots with our minds, and if our minds are moving in that direction, our bodies will definitely be on board.

Let's sprout some initiative and try something new.

Let's be creative and have some fun.

Let's take the first step with no fear.

Let's challenge ourselves.

It is time to wake the dream.

It is time.

Switch yourself on to new possibilities. There is a whole new world out there for you to discover. It is patiently waiting.

Here are some ideas.

What interests you?

Is it history? Is it music? Is it health? Is it travel?

Is it technology? Is it philanthropy?

Learn how to navigate search engines. Learn about "online" and don't be fearful.

Do you know you can tour your favourite art galleries online. You can be right there in the Uffizi Gallery in Florence immersed in Boticelli and Caravaggio. You can absorb Van Gogh in the Musée d'Orsay in Paris. How about New York's Museum of Modern Art or even London's Tate Gallery for Pollack and Monet?

The internet has opened up the universe. Understand it, ask for help, join tours.

Paint like a silent poet.

Make others feel.

And music?

Sing, dear seniors.

Sing loud and free and wobbly and in tune and out of tune.

There is no judgement.

Sing karaoke on your device.

Become a senior TikTok star. If you make millions, that is a plus. Oldies are trending.

(Look up what *trending* means).

Move fast—audiences are fickle.

Join clubs and societies and communities with similar interests.

Listen to opera online.

Register for a degree online.

Watch YouTube cooking classes, and replicate for friends or even for just yourself.

Start your own cooking trend.

Make things, be creative with your ideas. These ideas are uniquely yours. Own them.

And most important of all, stay connected to a community that will cheer you on and have your back. Find your tribe who believe you can do it—it may be one or many. Inspire others to do the same—they need you as much as you need them.

Think like John Glenn, who went to space as part of space shuttle mission STS-95 at seventy-seven.

Think like Minoru Saitō, who sailed solo and nonstop around the world at seventy-seven.

Think like Yuichiro Miura who reached the summit of Mount Everest at eighty.

Think like Nola Ochs who graduated from college at ninety-five.

And they say that sixty-five is the beginning of old age? Come on, dear seniors, who is telling us this? It is just an excuse.

We are mature, yes; we are wise, yes; we have life experience, yes.

So, throw chronological age in the bin. It only records the years you have been on this earth, nothing more.

Give things a go. There is no failure in trying.

Age is nothing but a state of mind.

A poem by Aztlanquill

There is an old saying that goes
You are only as old as you feel
Birthdays just tend to come and go
Only the thief of Time can steal.

Our looks, our health, our attitude
We desperately try to keep intact
And when we look in the mirror
We often ask, Who the hell is that?

Yes, we know that Time is that enemy
That we all try to make a friend
And we must never ever waste it
'Cause we will get older in the end

So live all of your life always
As if you are forever 21
And if you get to live to 90
Make sure you're always having fun

For age is but a feeling
You are as young as you feel
Make sure Time never takes
The things you treasure still

JUST A THOUGHT

Survival mode only prevents you from moving onwards and upwards.

SENIOR SAGE

Sore bones and slow gait and fuzzy memory and more fear are all part of where we are at. But as some seniors remind me, they are gloriously active and alive and proactive, even though they are older. Well done to them, but we are all not the same, and we have all had life experiences that can sometimes wither our being. The mind is *strong*—stronger than we will ever know. It is time even more so now to embrace and be grateful for what we have. We can always strive to make ourselves better.

Perfection Ain't Pretty

ARGHH! WHY DO OUR MOTHERS MAKE US FEEL THAT we need to be perfect? It is exhausting. No one cares. Perfection threatens people.

South African dinner parties in the early days of marriage took a week to prepare. We worked hard for perfection, for fear of an aftermath of gossip, comparison and judgement. We scrubbed our homes, marinated our meat and created ice bowls and fondues and cordon bleu. Our repertoire was magnificent in its perfection.

We carry over these ideals of perfection to our new Australian homes. Cutlery is polished, cut glass sparkles, candles are lit and floral arrangements blaze in colourful glory.

And everybody is miserable.

We are miserable, our guests are miserable.

We never see them again.

Do they not like us?

Do they not like our food?

Do they think I am too fat?

We are such idiots sometimes when we are younger. We duly observe, learn, relax, pour sauce from a bottle and scrape butter from a tub.

Everyone relaxes.
Everyone is content.
Conversation flows.
We make extraordinary lifelong friends.
Our family arrives for a visit.
They arrive early to maintain a one-year-old's sleep routine.
The house is messy.
The meal is unprepared.
The kitchen floor is grubby.
There is no soap or towel in the bathroom.
I haven't exercised.
I cannot find my hairbrush.
They arrive.
I still cannot find my hairbrush.
The family loves to see imperfection.
The visit is glorious and happy.
It makes us human.
They mend the garden gate.
They switch on the kettle.
They wash up.
We breathe.
They relax.
We are happy.
We do not need to be perfect.
Perfection and peace are not good partners. They are very conflicting.
Do your best, your very best, and leave the rest.
That is quite absolutely good enough.

JUST A THOUGHT

"If you look for perfection you will never be content."

– Leo Tolstoy

SENIOR SAGE

If you do your best, that is your best, and then you can try again to be better than your best. But this is only for your own satisfaction and has absolutely nothing to do with anyone or anything else.

Our Creation Is a Big Thing

FACT AND OBSERVATION.

A human is made from a mixture of cloudy, white liquid similar to raw egg or runny jelly that smells like bleach with cells that swim up to greet another cloudy sticky, gooey egg and—boom!—we are made. So, we are made from a splat of gooey liquid.

Of course, there is all the scientific explanation of what meets what and how, but if you really think about it, what looks like a slimy gob of mucous makes *us*.

And now the miracle begins, and it gets interesting.

It all seems to be very abstract from here. We know how the heart forms—it is an organ. But how does what goes into the heart get formed?

Is a soul dropped from above into that vacant space? Is it a reincarnated heart? Did it belong to someone else who was like us, or is it a fresh beginning for us to work on in our earthly journey? Who knows?

I have researched this subject and comments from all sides.

Some say…

"The soul is a developmental product. It depends on a certain sort of cultivation: including moral education" (H.G. Callaway, Temple University).

Others say...

"Life of a human being is confined within a century. On earth the soul goes together with a human life. After that it returns to God for its embodiment with Him. In other words, the soul was given to humans by the creator and returns to Him for its further perpetual processing" (Theodore Costopoulos, ELVAL Academy).

We can become dogmatic or confused in searching for the answers. We have philosophical opinions and scientific opinions and religious opinions and our very own opinions. And we don't really, really know. The big reveal will happen only when on the other side, I think.

It is not worth delving into different philosophies at this very moment, as it could fill the complete book. It is a long and fascinating subject. So, I'm going to leave it right there just to get you thinking.

JUST A THOUGHT

"You weren't an accident. You weren't mass produced. You aren't an assembly-line product. You were deliberately planned, specifically gifted, and lovingly positioned on the Earth by the Master Craftsman."

– Max Lucado

SENIOR SAGE

Let us be glorious in our creation. Let us treasure each moment and be so very grateful for life. Let us make each minute matter.

Where Is It Hiding?

I HAVE LUMPS AND BUMPS ALL OVER MY SKIN.

They must be bites as they itch like hell, but I am a bit befuddled because I am very efficient in applying citronella oil all over to ward off any creepy crawlies. They don't usually love the taste of my blood, preferring co-senior's O-Pos. He is always in the line of fire of mozzie stooker dive bombers. It is full onslaught.

It is different today. They are loving my blood group, and I am now the juicy morsel.

These days, I play hide-and-seek with little black specks whizzing past my retina. I think this is simply older age creeping up producing this flotilla of floaters, but maybe this time I am wrong, and it really is some little buzzing blighter ready to swoop in for its evening munchies.

Bugs and spiders and crawlies and biters and stingers are not my favourites. Actually, they are really my most "unfavourites".

"Hon!" I shout while fervently scrubbing off my "never comes off" lipstick before going to bed.

"There's a spider here!"

My knight in shining armour rushes in armed with a wet white towel ready to annihilate anything causing his damsel distress.

"Those guys are fine," he exclaims. "They are not dangerous or venomous. They are keeping an eye out for any real nasties that may attack." I am surprised at co-senior's knowledge.

I am not convinced, however, especially as they go undercover in darkness.

I really, really dislike spiders, especially the rather large, shiny, rear-their-head, funnel-web type found in Australia. These have made their mark internationally in vacation decision-making. Their reputations are infamous. They shout danger. I am very frightened of them, especially when one of these nasty visitors once reared up in aggressive defence as I opened the front door. It did, though, meet its demise under the weight of the full volume of an outdated Encyclopaedia Britannica.

Do you still want to visit Australia? Is it a yes?

Well, then, I won't start on the Irukandji jellyfish……

Back to the spider in the bedroom.

Co-senior inspects closely, and in collaboration we decide that it may just be OK to give this one a reprieve. I remain cautious.

As all seniors know, little nighttime bathroom sprints are necessary, urgent and frequent. My route is past the spider family squatting in the bedroom nook crevice. I am not happy to invade their gloomy grey space. I know that nighttime light is a no-no for "back to sleepy-byes", but I am an arachnophobe, and with a beam of light and a quick check-in, I may be able to score a double extermination and the hasty demise of a nightly buzzer who is puncturing my thinning sensitive skin.

With the fastest of flicks, the light illuminates, and there is nothing. Nothing! Where has the family gone? Are they snuggling in my bed, in the cupboard, having a quick midnight snack in the kitchen, up the sleeves of my pjs or in my shoes? I spring into action, flicking sheets and covers and pillows and undressing and dressing. I do it all. I find nothing.

With tentative purpose, I lay my head on the pillow and dream of clusters of spiders playing "Ring a Ring o' Roses" around the base of my bed. The sleep is restless.

Shrill, shrill.

The alarm wakes me from my restless sleep. I can't find my glasses, crawl out of bed and grumble and stumble to the bathroom. There seems to be a smudge in the bedroom crevice. I make a mental note to become more proficient at cleaning. Through the blur, I find my glasses on the chest of drawers, put them on and continue my walk.

With a quick backward glance, I tilt my head to reaffirm that the spider family has relocated to the neighbour's house. And there, in full glory, is the spider family back in their hidey-hole crevice.

They are now my creepy crawly army heroes. Tightly trapped in their web are two nasty, long-legged mosquitos, never again to breathe in carbon dioxide as they buzz around my head.

JUST A THOUGHT

"Spider: Remember when you threw a shoe at me and I fell behind the bed? I do too!"

SENIOR SAGE

Spiders are both predator and prey. They keep little insects under control and are preyed on by birds and other mammals. Sort of makes me feel sorry for them. They don't seem to have a good reputation.

The Mask Manoevour

THE SECOND WAVE HAS HIT, AND AFTER THE MASK, no-mask debate, we are now told that to prevent this contagion, we should all be donning our new accessory and all will be well.

We have added disposable masks to our monthly budget, and it is getting costly.

So, it is now time for innovation.

I research YouTube for instructions on how to create a homemade version. The plan is then to locate an inventive seamstress to produce an original version from the one-off fabric design purchased from an upmarket establishment in Los Angeles.

I do not sew. I never learned the skill and passionately admire those who can.

Donning my novice hat, I lay out a strip of fabric, attach two hair bands, fold it all back on itself and—voilà—job done.

But not done.

I can't see.

The mask is covering everything, even my new hairstyle that has had its first tint in months.

So, back to the drawing board.

The next attempt is the sock-into-mask design. By cutting off the toe and sewing up the side and inverting and cutting little incisional arms on the sides, once again I am in business.

But not to be. The heel section of the bisected sock has stretched, creating an unusual Pinocchio effect, which is most unbecoming. And aside from that, co-senior is unhappy, as I have had a few attempts at this innovative version and he now has no socks.

Third time lucky as I rummage through tight-weave scraps for my new attempt. The latest find is glorious in its originality. I can have a banana accessory day or a unicorn day or even a Barbie day. It could even go viral (I said *viral* not *virus*; we need to be clear about that) and with a complete lack of sewing ability, I could become the next new TikTok phenomena.

These versions don't exactly seem to be hitting the mark.

So back again to YouTube, and the discovery that yes, a mask can be made from underpants, and yes, a mask can even be made out of a bra. At last, I feel I am donating at least something to the recycled face-protection movement. I am doing the right thing. I am not only protecting myself but am giving full protection to co-senior as well.

The bra size, however, has increased in isolation. This is a bad but also a good thing. The good is that there is now enough bra fabric to protect all family members plus the neighbours and the neighbour's neighbours as well. It is a full street prophylactic.

Oh well, didn't we say that we are all in this together?

JUST A THOUGHT

"A mask tells us more than a face."

– *Oscar Wilde*

SENIOR SAGE

You will never forget what you had for breakfast and what you had for breakfast last week while in this mask-wearing stage. Remember to wash your reusable masks and listen to the experts. It says more about the person wearing the mask than those who don't.

Fluffer Doodle in the Bank

I HAVE FOUND A SLIMMING BAR THAT SPEEDS UP metabolism. Now this is a find!

These bars are scrumptious and advertise boldly that they will keep us full and fabulous. They include, however, some unusual ingredients that I do not recognise. Seeing they are from a reputable pharmaceutical company, I trust that the experts must know what they are doing. At last, I can pass on the stash of sweet snacks bought on a whim in my last grocery shop outing.

Today is a big day.

I am out of the cage. Co-senior has wrapped me in cotton wool this year. He says he is keeping me safe. So safe that I have almost forgotten how to drive.

I sometimes think he has too….. but I am excited. Independence, at last, for the first time in months.

Actually, this is merely a trip to the bank, not, unfortunately, a fancy restaurant or upmarket boutique. But I need to be grateful as it is an outing, nevertheless.

I wear a mask and tie a knot in the hooks around the ears to ensure that the droplet protection is less airy. My adjustment, however, has caused breathing problems, so I return to the car to unpick the knots. Unpicking the knot on the left side is simple, but the right side is being difficult. It is mangled in its stranglehold. So, I am now back in the bank with my lopsided appendage that hides my new bright red lipstick that is screaming for attention.

It is lunchtime, but I am not hungry. The nutritional bars have fulfilled their promise. A little secret—I did rather overindulge, seeing they were healthy, but added in a healthy portion of a new bean stew recipe I had wanted to make for yonks and now had.

At this point, I perform a circular reconnaissance and decide that maybe, just maybe, the bubbles invading my abdomen could have a *liiiiittle* release so that I am not uncomfortable when it is my turn to front the bank manager. Nonchalantly, I tighten and release—and let go.

A resounding, booming-gas-explosion cacophony of sound ricochets back from the newly renovated vacuous banking space.

I immediately turn to the unsuspecting victim behind, nose upturned and lament loudly….

"Arghh, someone has farted!"

I know this is mean, very mean.

The non-offender is looking very embarrassed, but I know I am not winning. Accusing eyes surround me, boring into my conscience.

I then begin a *Riverdance* spectacle, jumping and tapping and beating on the polished floor in the hope that the sound could have been mistaken for maybe a practice session of my new dancing skill.

Nah, this also isn't working.

The long queue in their "iso" outing is now beginning to enjoy my embarrassment, and the giggles start, growing louder and louder, fuelling my humiliation. I have been caught red-handed, and I have to now wear this mantle of shame.

Note to myself…

Stop eating bars that note in the fine print that they have a laxative effect on overconsumption. And stop experimenting on vegan and beans.

It could have been worse. A few minutes later, and I would have been in the bank manager's tiny office. I don't think I would have received any sympathy in my plea for mortgage relief as the meeting time would have been severely curtailed in pursuit of fresh air. And there would be no one to blame. It would be just the two of us.

Aah, only a lesson to be learned. No more bars, no more outings, no more spending and no more bean stew recipes. Just a good daily dose of Lactobacillus mixed in with a healthy fermented kombucha, and all will be "tickety-boo".

JUST A THOUGHT

"If you fart while wearing a thong, does it whistle?"

– *Minions on Pinterest*

SENIOR SAGE

Muscles become weaker as you get older. You don't build much muscle after a certain age. Power up those "underground muscles". You surely don't want to become the entire percussion section.

Keep It Alive

THE FOLLOWING IS NOT MY ORIGINAL AND IS CREDITED back to Reddit and posted by Bushwacker61, HDCikky,u/pennywise32, the ministry of troll affairs and countless others.

It is out there and has done the rounds many times. You may have read it before, and now you may be minus a chapter in this book as it is nothing new.

You may be irritated as you crave original material.

You may be compelled to write an average review—please don't.

I can't credit all who have reposted this everywhere, BUT I am still going to tell the story. Be patient—I will tell you why at the end of the chapter.

The Black Bra (as told by a woman)

I had lunch with two of my unmarried friends.

One is engaged,

One is a mistress

and I have been married for 20+ years.

We were chatting about our relationships and decided to amaze our men by greeting them at the door wearing a black bra, stiletto heels and a mask over our eyes.

We agreed to meet in a few days to exchange notes.

Here's how it all went.

My engaged friend:

"The other night when my boyfriend came over, he found me with a black leather bodice, tall stilettos and a mask. He saw me and said, 'You are the woman of my dreams. I love you.' Then we made passionate love all night long."

The mistress:

"Me too! The other night I met my lover at his office, and I was wearing a raincoat, under it only the black bra, heels and mask over my eyes. When I opened the raincoat, he didn't say a word, but he started to tremble, and we had wild sex all night."

Then I had to share my story:

"When my husband came home, I was wearing the black bra, black stockings, stilettos and a mask over my eyes. When he came in the door and saw me, he said,

'**What's for dinner, Zorro?**'"

Is this you? Is number three you? Are you still being noticed, or have you blended into an insignificant daily routine?

Keep it alive, dear seniors. Introduce the unexpected—in marriage, in friendship, in relationships, in family, in life.

Remain curious and interesting.

Life will remain so much more fun.

JUST A THOUGHT

"If you do nothing unexpected, nothing unexpected happens."

– Fay Weldon

SENIOR SAGE

Keep it alive, love a routine, but don't sink into the suburban mundane. There is still so much out there to explore. Go find it, and it will find you.

Money Money Money

MONEY. WHO WANTS TO EVEN TALK ABOUT IT?

Unfortunately, as seniors we have to think about it and budget and live within our means.

We remain silent about the "hole in the bucket".

We don't want to feel embarrassed or judged but are instinctively aware that most are in the same boat. We are sinking or surviving together.

We spend less, worry more, and identify and remember specials from the newspaper inserts.

We don't hanker for possessions anymore. We hanker for extra years to create memories that can be sustained well into our final days.

Marie Kondo has become our new best friend. We de-clutter, throw away, donate and sell.

We are stressed when stuff clambers onto our desks and into our cupboards. We have no clear pathway to think.

We want to plan, and we want simplicity and clarity to work out what is now pushing our buttons.

Our health system and medical innovations are keeping us alive, and we love it. Our social security doesn't.

We spread our pot of gold around to create financial security. Bank interest has plummeted, share markets are volatile and unreliable, dividends are diminishing. Battle lines between countries and taxes that ensue damage the economy.

What was trending beautifully yesterday is sweeping the floor today.

In our planning, bank interest, share dividends and smart investments would have saved the day. But not so now. Everything now seems risky.

Costs are increasing, and our kids are becoming anxious with the looming threat that the financial burden of their parents lands on them and stretches them also way too far.

It is tough.

The whimsical ads of "grey foxes" driving through picturesque mountains, drinking champagne on deserted beaches while riding camels are a myth. It is "hard yakka" out there at the moment, and we all have to be on our game.

Being a senior and coming from a premise of authentic experience, this is what I have found.

(I am not an expert, so speak to someone who is. I am merely an expert at being a senior, and sometimes collaborative discussions and solutions work for the benefit of all.)

We have choices.

We can:

1. live off our savings
2. increase our income
3. reduce our costs
4. apply for a pension or………

5. get involved in some ambiguous multi-level scheme, spruiked by various nationalities promising waterfront mansions and Ferraris in the blink of an eye.

This may help:

- Read and learn.
- Find a mentor who has been successful, note what they do, and copy. (Nothing wrong with that.)
- Both in a partnership should be fully aware of the finances. (If one in a partnership goes, the other partner becomes exceedingly vulnerable.)
- Be on top of your finances; be aware of your debt.
- Track your shares in your share portfolio (if you have shares).
- Pay off credit cards, pay off credit cards, pay off credit cards. Paying interest is so wasteful.
- Only have one credit card. Spending becomes less addictive.
- Check your statements, and notice when some vague charge appears. (Sometimes entries do not appear familiar as some companies invoice out in different names, so remember that before querying.)
- Be very wary of financial advisors unless they come highly recommended and reviewed by many with sound ratings. There are wonderful wordsmiths out there who will promise you the world with their experience and financial advisor knowledge. They want to make you money as it makes them more money. However, if they lose all your savings, they will still be dining out on a Friday night schmoozing

with their latest asset-rich client. They are not your family or friend—it's just a j.o.b.

I know it may appear that I have a jaded perspective. I do.

My highly intelligent and finance-savvy mum was sucked into the charms of a bright-eyed broker. He mentioned to all his friends that her portfolio was a ripper and puffed and preened in his ability to search out risky, high-return investments. She lost most of that portfolio, and in her senior years struggled to climb back on the profitable ladder again.

And then again, I judge equally. There are some wonderful advisors out there—do your homework.

- B.u.d.g.e.t.
  Nobody likes to budget. But how do you know if you have enough if you don't know what you are spending? You will be most surprised.
- Takeout coffees—approximately $4.00–4.50 *every day* for just one cup = $1,640 per annum. That is a trip to see the family who lives on the other side of the world.
- How about telephone bills? Check them carefully. You may have an older number hiding between other numbers. If you have been on a cruise, even with appropriate plan, you will have a rude awakening when you discover international waters are not regarded as a country. You will need to plan a huge E-bay, Facebook, Gumtree, Craigslist sale on your return to dry land. And we seniors do love cruising!
- Missed payments could show on your credit report, and then you have the joyful experience of trying

to convince the bank manager that it was merely an oversight and you are a perfectly sound credit risk.

- Domain names and hosting services and streaming services and subscriptions and everything else that is seamlessly debited monthly from your account may appear small. But believe me, they add up. I am embarrassed to say we found that we had been paying for the hosting of an email address of a past employee for over twelve months, never knowing what the charge was for on the account and not knowing how to query.
- Ask your kids (if you have kids) to add you as an additional member on their family plans, and suddenly you are up to date on the latest music. It doesn't cost you anything.
- Double cook dinner to have enough for leftovers tomorrow.
- Go to bulk-bill medical services (this may only apply to Australia), and find a doctor you really like and trust, and you will save extensively.
- Learn about mortgage offset accounts. Shop around for better interest rates, and dig your heels in until the powers that be listen. I know this can be tricky as lenders want financials, and there may be no regular monthly income. Pay-back security could be hard to prove.
- Talk to other seniors, and share knowledge.

I'm not an expert, dear seniors, but I am a senior, and in the process of being authentic, all I know is that sharing a banana when you used to eat the whole fruit salad can be demoralising, unusual and uncomfortable as we get older.

In the isolation situation we are presently in, people are struggling and are frustrated and angry.

Mortgages are on hold, credit card providers are being beseeched for clemency and people are shifting backwards and forwards from bank statement to bank statement. Queues are overpopulating social security centres, and people are downhearted.

However, I am sure we have more than so many others, and now that we have time to think, we should be able to do some planning.

Keep your eye open for those who are really struggling. Sometimes their game face is not revealing their actual situation.

Pay forward if you can.

It's a funny thing, this money. It is meant to make the world go round. But, if we endeavour to help our fellow human beings, asking nothing in return, karma always seems to come home to visit.

The next lotto ticket draw could be yours, and you could be financially free.

It is not a pipe dream.

It happened to my father-in-law, brought up in an orphanage, eating gruel and corn.

He won the lotto.

He bought a car.

He won the lotto again.

He bought a house.

My father-in-law, Johnny. He was a good man.

JUST A THOUGHT

"Money makes the world go round."

– *Cabaret, 1960*

SENIOR SAGE

You can't worship both money and God, and my belief is that at some stage in our humanity the time will come for you to make the choice.

Bless the Millennials

ALL HAIL TO OUR HERO MILLENNIALS AND EMERGENCY services. You have turned up right when we need you the most.

You are our present-day heroes, not caped but masked up in your protective headgear and equipment.

You have showed up with superhuman bravery and stamina.

You have swabbed us and have shown respect for our weakness.

You have reassured us and held our hands.

You are the "only" when there is no one else in the room.

Kindness and empathy are tattooed in your heart.

Yours are the beautiful faces of human kindness.

You have left your own families and isolated to keep them safe while you have become our families, keeping us sane.

You are there in the centre of essential services, packing shelves and delivering groceries and staying in control in ambulances and ICU.

You teach our children at the risk of your own.

You are showing up, and we are embracing.

You have become sympathetic, and you are breathing out calm.

We watch you and know you have the future right there in your hands.

You have stepped forward, you have found your place in time, you are getting on with things and we admire you.

You are our Oscar winner heroes.

You have always been there. We just haven't taken the time to stop and notice and understand.

We are on opposite sides of life, but we are not that different.

We were young once but a different kind of young.

We were taught differently, and we think differently because of our influences.

But now we have time to think.

We have time to stop.

We have time and inclination to reach out and touch and hold each other's hands across our huge generational divide.

We can learn from each other moving forward and try to be better.

We will stop and notice.

We will be gentle.

We will listen.

We will *love.*

JUST A THOUGHT

"Sometimes you'll hold on really hard and realize there is no choice but to let go. Acceptance is a quiet, small room. Trusting yourself means living out what you already know to be true. Every last one of us can do better than give up."

– *Adunola Adeshola*

"When you come out of the storm, you won't be the same person who walked in. That's what this storm's all about."

– *Haruki Murakami*

SENIOR SAGE

It's time to stop being critical and angry with each other. It is time to build bridges of understanding and listen to both sides of the life cycle. We all can learn so much from the past and the future.

The Knockers Are Having a Freedom Festival

I DON'T KNOW HOW TO DRESS ANYMORE. I HAVE forgotten what goes with what. The same trousers and top say hello every morning, and we embrace like long-lost comfortable lovers.

Everything is now in body-part heaven, especially the slight angle in my spine, which has not been locked, for a couple of months, in a brace of bra fasteners. My knockers are swaying in jubilation, having a veritable freedom festival.

Let's just be clear here. We are not lazy, are we, seniors? We just don't see anyone in our daily routine, so why enforce a stranglehold if not needed? Why should we pretty up in the underwear department? Who cares if our bits are sitting pretty in place or having a conversation with our belly button?

I actually don't know where my favourite bra is, and to be quite honest, I can't remember which bra was my favourite. It is probably nestling comfortably in house arrest with an evening outfit and some sparkly shoes.

At some point I am going to have to go on a search party. Invitations will arrive again, and I will tentatively have to venture out to maybe, just maybe, celebrate an anniversary dinner or some such occasion in a non-cluster suburb.

Seasons have changed while we have been housebound, so summer gear is starting to relay with winter gear in the "exchange of season" cupboard with an occasional "pop up" dotted in the cupboard not wanting to say good-bye just yet.

Co-senior and I decide that we now feel safer, and we can therefore venture out to the indoor pool at our local gym to have a swim. Lockdown has stimulated the creative juices to continue with my senior storytelling journey, but the downside is that I am sitting around far more than I should be. So, off we go to rectify this.

It is winter and too c..c..cold at the gym to be undressed.

I am not a fan of a wet floor in a public ladies' changeroom. I am a germaphobe as you already know. Warts, streptococcus, staphylococcus and more conditions I can't pronounce may be lurking.

We arrive at so said pool in our bathing costumes, prepped and ready. At this stage we are not aware that we are a little less prepped than we should be.

Floating in the cool pool water feels exhilarating. Our limbs are happy as we stretch them further than they should go. Our lymph is happy as at last it has woken up after a long stagnant rest.

The air is bracing when we jump out. We know this time that we have to embrace our men's and ladies' change rooms as we have promised ourselves a rewarding, warm cappuccino on the way home. The alternative is pneumonia. We pat ourselves on the back as we have come prepared to change and boast even further that we did this without even a checklist.

We are not prepared.

"Sweetheart, is my bra in your bag?"

Co-senior comes up empty-handed.

"Hon, are my undies in your bag?"

I come up empty-handed.

And now the debate ensues. Who is going to do the cappuccino run? My dress is see-through, and co-senior's shorts are too short, so it is risky business whichever way we look at it.

I win—doesn't the queen always win?

Co-senior, my gallant hero, minces into the coffee shop to ensure that there is no peekaboo. He does get some very strange looks, especially when bumping into an old friend who thinks he has lost his nuts. Well, he sort of has, as they imposter Newton's Cradle.

Our day ends up with our hot cappuccino reward, and we regard this as a success.

Our bits have had an unconfined outing, and a note to myself that it is time to play my own game of peekaboo when I get home to find my bra escapee in the underwear drawer.

JUST A THOUGHT

"Whenever you're sitting across from some important person, always picture him sitting there in a suit of long, red underwear. That's the way I always operated in business."

– Joseph P. Kennedy

SENIOR SAGE

My mum always told me to go out in good underwear just in case I had an accident. Sorry, Mum, I forgot this time. It's an age thing.

Stop

I HAD TO PULL CO-SENIOR DOWN OFF THE ROOF THIS morning.

I have to admit I have been bullying a tad as he is refusing to share "coffee time" with his beloved on awakening.

This has been our cosy custom for our whole married life. We have even expanded his skills to negotiating the knobs and spouts of the new Nespresso machine, and he has become rather adept in this area. He is now reading brochures on weird and wonderful bean extractions from all over the world. I love being his experimental guinea pig, but I am, however, a "coffee snob", so I have dented his self-esteem, rather similar to "Goldilocks and the three bears".

The coffee is either too hot or too cold, too bitter or too sweet, too strong or too weak.

Poor co-senior is not winning.

However, with much trial and effort, he is at last on top of his game to such an extent that there are no more outings to the local cafe. In my estimation, he is number one barista, and nothing can compare.

Co-senior informed me last week that he wouldn't be sharing a coffee with me anymore, as it is irritating his digestive system. I love it irritating *my* digestive system as it saves on my weekly grocery budget of prunes and fibre.

However, it isn't so much the no-coffee routine he is now following that is irking me but the lack of companionship in sipping and planning our day together.

After expounding on all the benefits of coffee, such as it helps lose weight (although co-senior doesn't need to lose an inch), contains antioxidants (which we all need at the moment), reduces prostate cancer risk (well, doc says all is happy and healthy), protects your brain, brightens your mood and a host of other things.

"Sweetheart, you need more energy. Coffee will kick-start your day!"

I rapidly discover that I should have taken these coffee attributes far more seriously when promoting them, as I am now extricating him from the ceiling when caffeine and resultant adrenaline rush kicks in.

And then the day explodes, and I can't find co-senior. One moment he is sweeping leaves outside, the next he has washed all the windows, taken out all the garbage, written twenty emails, gone to gym, called a page of business prospects, gone grocery shopping, collected the post,washed the car.....

So now my rhetoric changes.

"Sweetheart, you just need to relax."

No wonder poor co-senior is confused.

I don't have to worry.

Adrenaline has now worn off, and he is slumped on his favourite couch, mouth open and eyes shut, quite impervious to instructions that Nagging Nelly has been directing at him at the beginning and end of the day.

I am delighted to see him burned out—not in a nasty way, of course.

I never see co-senior relaxing.

As the key turns in the door on my return home from anywhere, co-senior jumps up and busies himself with anything that is in reach. I notice and feel guilty but keep my lips zipped as I would much rather observe than participate at this time of day. I'd rather find some "me" time than concern myself with housekeeping routines.

However, I have noticed that co-senior is not his sparkling self of late. He is drowning in domesticity.

"Are you OK?"

Co-senior nods.

I continue watching my prime-time rubbish as I hear him bustling in the background.

"Are you sure you are OK?"

I am now feeling very guilty.

"Why don't you sit here with me and switch off for a while, and we can do the dishes together later?"

"I can't," replies co-senior.

"And why not?"

"I just feel so guilty when I take a break!"

With a gnawing conscience, I jump up from my embedded laziness to help.

I gently coerce co-senior to the couch and Al Jazeera.

While I grab our morning plates and immerse my fingers in hardened egg, I know that I have put my oxygen mask on first, my energy is full, and it is now time for me to help co-senior put on his and uncomplicate the act of rest in his mind.

JUST A THOUGHT

"Rest until you feel like playing, then play until you feel like resting, period. Never do anything else."

– Martha Beck

SENIOR SAGE

Burnout is going to be in your future, I promise, if you don't take time to rest. Not only is it smart but it propels you to even greater heights. Give yourself permission to rest—it is not laziness.

Angels and Demons

I WAS QUITE HAPPY TO BE A GOODY-GOODY TODAY.

Many in the supermarket hadn't quite "got with the programme". Social distancing was nonexistent, and for fear of wiping out someone with my trolley or handbag, I steered myself widely around each participant, holding my breath and acquiring a serious case of blood-pressure spike.

There were a few ways that this situation could have been handled.

I could have politely done a "jump to the left" whenever I passed, but that would have been unfortunate for the tuna cans that were right in my line of fire, or I could have lashed out with verbal abuse, which may have been unfortunate for me, as everyone's tempers are a bit frayed at the moment and I might have been on the very pointy end of someone else's tirade.

But, in my bubble of awareness, what I did notice was how incredibly selfish people can be. Firstly, we are seniors, and stats have provided the information that we are weaklings as far as this disease is concerned and that it is playing games with our psyche.

For some, though, it seems like there is a moment of glee observing our predicament, as they feel we are the entitled generation and if we are removed, there is more space in the universe for them.

Maybe I should bring my tape measure next time to educate on what 1.5 metres should look like.

Then there are the coughers and splutterers who are showing off their skills at body contusion as they wrap themselves around the plastic dividers meant to protect any vagrant spittle. Their eyes are swollen from nasal congestion, and they sneeze and cough with no regard, right onto the EFTPOS machine that the following unsuspecting customer presses unawaredly, only to forget that the simple act of straightening their glasses could land up as an induced coma merely to keep them alive.

And then while exiting promptly, I overhear a manager in the adjacent shop advising very loudly that he really should not be at work as he has a sore throat and temperature and isn't feeling good.

Oh, how grateful am I that I have been moving my little legs in the neighbourhood walks during this crisis since I am extremely adept at doing a trolley run at pace and fleeing to the carpark to protect myself once more in my motor vehicle, lathered with handwash and a washed-down takeaway coffee?

Back tracking a bit, this was always not so.

When we first exited our cloistered security, we were all beautifully behaved, wore our masks like good responsible citizens and had to speak just a little louder as lip reading through masks needed x-ray vision and was now a thing of the past. Fellow citizens assisted us seniors with grocery shops and postal drops, and this little space in the busyness of life showed some real compassion.

But now, months into this very unusual situation, we have become frustrated and impatient and our angel wings have become muddied. Deep inside, I am sure we all are our own inner angels, but it is now taking some soul searching to remain calm and lovely when our spirit is being harshly challenged. We can choose to be angels or demons, and hopefully being kind is our fall back in these situations. It will surely serve us so much better when life is back on an even keel.

JUST A THOUGHT

"He who does not see the angels and devils in the beauty and malice of life will be far removed from knowledge, and his spirit will be empty of affection."

– Khalil Gibran

SENIOR SAGE

We are all born simply pure, and then our environment and circumstances take over. How beautiful this world would be if we were able to go back to the start.

Bookending Infinity

WARNING—ONE NEEDS TO BE INTELLECTUAL TO understand this subject fully. So, forgive me if this is just a simple authentic take on the situation.

I am sitting in my car, practicing meditation while waiting to collect a friend from the station.

All I can focus on is "spatial infinity"—an unusual thought for a Thursday afternoon.

I am thinking how Christians believe that the world was created in seven days by God, and scientists believe that it was all a "Big Bang" and there is a scientific answer.

Some of us mere earthlings try to understand the dark foreverness prior to Creation and then try to understand post-earthly life and where exactly we are going to go when jettisoned back into eternal black.

Nobody can confirm anything for us.

We are little dots in this humongous earthly space, jammed in tight between the two "infinities."

The little lifeline between the bookends is small. We live this tiny lifeline to the beat of fast and furious. Sometimes we realise too late that we never made a difference, and will we be judged as such by our Creator when the dark returns?

Infinity... life... infinity.

Do people even think about this? Or are we all particles of one, fused together again in our next spiritual journey or rebirth?

Sir Martin Rees, a Royal Society Research Professor holding the title of Astronomer Royal, comments in his book *Just Six Numbers: The Deep Forces that Shape the Universe.* He states,

> At the start of the twenty-first century, we have identified six numbers that seem especially significant. Two of them relate to the basic forces; two fix the size and overall "texture" of our Universe and determine whether it will continue forever; and two more fix the properties of space itself.
>
> Taken together, these six numbers have been described as a kind of "recipe" for our universe. If any of them varied more than slightly, or if they were not "fine-tuned" to one another, the universe and life we know it could not exist. The odds of these constants all having their specific values as a result of mere chance are extremely small—nearly zero.
>
> Therefore, the existence of a Cosmic Designer must be considered. [5]

Hey, he is a scientist, and he said it!

Are we getting closer to understanding this meaning of life?

It's hard for scientists. They need definitive answers. I saw it firsthand with my own father, who believed there was a scientific explanation for everything.

We may never in our lifetime *have* proof, but we can every one of us *feel* proof if we dig deep and feel hard enough.

Our Cosmic Designer will be right there beside us, and we will just know.

We will face a reality of eternity and love and soul connection.

Infinity… Life… Eternity.

That sounds more like it. How about you?

JUST A THOUGHT

"Figuring God into the world of science is a nebulous task. What happens when observers of the fact-based natural world must come to terms with the faith-based spirituality of the mystical world?"

– *Tavish Nanda*

SENIOR SAGE

I suppose when you know, you just know. Infinity is related to anything that cannot be counted or measured. Eternity relates to the state of being timeless.

Valentine's Day

VALENTINE'S DAY IN A BOARDING SCHOOL IS A veritable shame-filling nightmare.

Expectant murmurs ripple through the school corridors weeks before the actual day.

We pray in anticipation that we are on the receiving end of a rose-patterned card filled with eloquent amorous words, even if from the pimpled masculine adolescent at the adjoining school.

The pretty, sexy classmates are always nonchalant recipients. They can pick and choose their following.

But it is a lottery pick for the rest. We are lost in the peripheral. We will accept anything in our desperation for teenage popularity. We will even stoop right down low in our anguish and send one off to ourselves.

Our letter monitor calls out the names of anyone in receipt of mail on the day. We pretend we are not fussed while concealing our crossed fingers under the plastic school tablecloths.

Sometimes we are lucky; sometimes we are not.

The popular card holders preen for a few days about the invisible loves of their lives, while we discuss the next maths test to prove we are not rattled.

And then the sun sets, and the day is done, and we can breathe again till next year.

Valentine's Day still rears its head again in our senior years, albeit a commercial and profitable calendar date for retailers selling anything red.

I am not sure if it is a romantic notion anymore but rather a touch of loving remembrance that a friend, partner, loved one is still there thinking of us, and that is complete in its remembrance.

Co-senior has been on the other end of hints and tips as February 14 looms in the future. (I know it is a throwback to missing out in the junior days, as you all know that being left out is my thing.)

I have hinted that sexy lacy underwear always gives a thrill. Red sexy underwear, although unusual, is even more exotic.

Co-senior flits off to the lingerie shop. He is always good at expediting subliminal instructions.

He fearlessly mingles amongst frilly Simone Perele and Kiki de Montparnasse and names that reek of exotic.

He receives a few suspicious glares, especially having donned his black three-ply mask. Is he a stalker? Does he love the feel of silk on his body?

"Can I help you?" the boutique manager enquires.

"Oh, yes," replies co-senior. "I would like to purchase a lingerie set for my wife for Valentine's Day."

There is a collective *aahhhhh*

"How sweet!" "Isn't he cute?"

"I wish my partner would buy a set for me."

"Can you girls help me?" (Yes, I did say *girls* as everyone looked like a girl—he could have been wrong, of course.)

"Of course," they all reply in unison.

Co-senior is in his element, wandering through lace and silk with a team of scouters in tow, looking for the perfect set for the love of his life.

"What size are you looking for?"

Co-senior can be a bit politically incorrect, so excuse us here.

He holds up his hand and bunches his palm in the shape of a tennis ball.

"About this size," he says.

"We know just the set," they reply as they rush off to the expensive rack.

"34B, that will be perfect," as they swoon in desire of the same package arriving with their coffee on Valentine's Day morning.

Co-senior is ecstatic. This is certainly going to be a winner, and he is having a winner of a day.

The parcel is gloriously wrapped, and Valentine's Day arrives in its expectation.

I untie the ruby red ribbon around the ruby red wrapping paper around the ruby red, lace-ravishing French underwear.

"Put it on, put it on," urges co-senior, ecstatic in his success.

"Oh, thank you, thank you, sweetheart. How about I try it on and model it tonight when we have more time?" having observed 34B glaring through the wrapping.

"And I really don't want to spill coffee on such a beautiful set."

Co-senior is glowing; he has got it right. Isn't he a smarty pants?

On his departure, I completely de-robe the elegant tissue paper to discover the teensiest, weeniest lacy set peering back.

I sigh in relief as the boutique name is emblazoned all over the box. I call in desperation to enquire whether they have the same set in, dare I say it, the plus section.

"Of course," chirps the manager, "we don't discriminate in any way in this store."

Thank goodness for political correctness. This has saved the day.

With a hot foot back to the store and a quick exchange, I rush home and stand at the top of the stairs as I hear the key in the front door.

Co-senior freezes, a huge grin on his face. He feels victorious. Such a clever boy.

He knows his partner very well after years of marriage. He knows the size of his woman.

"Oh, my darling, you look sensational! I knew I was getting quite the right size when I purchased a small. You are simply quite gorgeous!"

I think I will leave it right there.

JUST A THOUGHT

"Happy Valentine's Day to myself. I love you."

– *www.livelifehappy.com*

SENIOR SAGE

This chapter could be oh so politically incorrect in gender expression, but it is senior authenticity, and really, who cares about the cards; it is the words that matter.

We Have an A cappella Going

CO-SENIOR HAS BEEN COMPLAINING ABOUT HIS EARS for a while now.

He is convinced that he has become a candle manufacturer in his ear canal warehouse.

We have researched and attempted ear wax removal via a variety of methods.

I suggested that we take our chances with ear candling, which felt very modern and new age. But, as our hands shake more these days, we felt the risk would override the results.

Then we were on a mission to find the best ear wax "goodymaggigies" that would miraculously dissolve the problem to create a free flow of auditory waves.

Despite focused attention and use of all these potions, co-senior's situation is getting worse.

It is now time for medical intervention. He is ripe and ready for a waxy boulder explosion from these tiny orifices.

The doc, however, advises that there is nothing, nudda, naught wax to be seen, and this home-remedy experimentation was most probably harming, not helping.

Then, next step in the ear saga was that co-senior advised that there seemed to be a buzzing in his ears, sort of like the buzz from the heavy electrical cables that were erected next to our last rental home. I gently reminded him that it was called tinnitus and not tendonitis.

I had also experienced a moth ear invasion many years back, so knew that feeling, and it didn't sound same, same. Mine was more like a squadron of military aircraft next to my brain, not a gentle, irritating buzz.

Co-senior hasn't been a heavy metal listener, and there are no "big bangs" that caused ear damage in his youth, so was this just a slow, aging ear symptom that we would all most likely be experiencing when it was our turn?

This hearing problem, however, is now providing its own vocabulary, and our conversations are becoming rather unusual.

Me:	"Hon, what would you like for dinner?"
Co-senior:	"What do you mean, I'm a sinner?"
Me:	"This is driving me mad."
Co-senior:	"No, I am not sad."
Me:	"You make the best of what's around."
Co-senior:	"You make the best hot stew around."
Me:	"Can you lay the table?"
Co-senior:	"Cannula able?"
Me:	"It's windy today."
Co-senior:	"No, it's Thursday."
Me:	"I think I have acute angina."
Co-senior:	"I think so too."

Our new language is developing.

I do feel sad for co-senior since it makes him feel unstable and messes with his confidence.

I do, however, notice that many of our friends have little gadgets nestling in their ears, and they are all doing oh so fine. In fact, possibly even finer, as they can selectively control the on and offs of occasional nags.

So, I connected with my most informative online best friend, Lecturer Google, to work out first steps in solving or assisting co-senior in this ear-evolution process. And I discovered quite simply that this is just the process we go through as our days become shorter.

We need to check it out.

We need to have a hearing test. There are countless gadgets and devices that can enhance hearing. We will be right as rain.

In the meantime, there is an a cappella of "I can't hear you" going on in our household.

We talk in code and interpretations, and we belt out our favourite songs with no fear of reprisal. Nobody can hear us anyway, and we can't really hear each other either.

From me upstairs in the bathroom: "There's a bad moon on the rise." From co-senior downstairs in the study: "There's a bathroom on the right." And we are both proudly, gloriously and loudly in a cappella disjointed harmony.

JUST A THOUGHT

"And before my Soul took me to task, I was hard of hearing. I heard only tumult and uproar. But now I am all ears listening to the silence and its choirs singing the hymns of time, intoning the praises of the firmament, revealing the secrets of the invisible."

– *Khalil Gibran*

SENIOR SAGE

I don't know what would be worse—not being able to see or not being able to hear. Let's take a moment and honour all the incredible humans who cannot see or cannot hear. What an example to all of us that in their adjustment to their physical challenges, they are still extraordinarily and gloriously complete.

We've Lost the Angels and Baby Jesus

WE'VE LOST THE ANGELS AND BABY JESUS.

They are always kept on the top shelf in our storage unit, reigning over our earthly archives and ready for a Christmas outing.

"Can you please move the box over there on the left?" I ask co-senior.

"We have personal on the left and tax documents on the right. Maybe they have found a new home this year, slipped down amongst the fluffy toucan or unused amplifier."

Co-senior and I have disappeared amongst dusty cardboard boxes, collapsing plastic tubs and forgotten bikes and golf clubs in our new downsized storage unit.

We could always find everything when we rented a half-full, overpriced unit next door, but as you know, getting older means slashing the budget, and storage downsizing is one of the casualties.

"What's in this box?"

"And why isn't it facing forward and marked?" I ask in frustration.

Doesn't everyone get it?

If the boxes are properly marked and facing the same way and not in front of a cupboard that opens, then everything that needs to be found will be found.

Co-senior is gracefully compliant, despite my strident tone. He pivots the back of the box to the front. We have inspected every other box in the unit, and I pray that this time we will hit the jackpot.

The box is marked "General", which elicits the need for a box cutter.

Co-senior adeptly strikes through the masking tape to reveal.....

English essays and army gear from the kid's teenage years.

"Why are we paying storage for English essays and army gear?" I ask co-senior. "Why are the kids not claiming their stuff? Why are we holding onto their memories as well as ours?"

Silence.

We tape up the box and go in search for the marker that has dropped between the boxes.

This box needs more detailed description.

There is no light in the storage unit. We have locked our phones (with the flashlight app) away in the car for fear of "dump on a box and forget which box" situation. But, to no avail. The marking pen has disappeared, and the box remains in the nondescript "general" category.

And we still cannot find the elusive angels and baby Jesus.

“Did one wing fall off and we threw the angels away?” I ask co-senior.

“Or did we loan baby Jesus to our smallest grandchild to pop under her pillow when she slept over and was scared?”

“No idea,” says co-senior as he clambers over cardboard.

We are at a loss. We surely wouldn’t have discarded them in our move. It’s like throwing away our old school Bible; you don’t chuck these “if you throw away you will get into trouble” kind of things. It could be bad Feng shui.

We drive home empty-handed.

Our local supermarket has been running a promotion to collect “Ooshies”. This little figurine is going off. We have enthusiastically been approached by all our grandchildren to collect the prized items. This we have done, but we are aware that we are required to be extremely diligent in sharing out equally so as not to display any favouritism. The promotion is on again this month, and—Geronimo!—one of the “Ooshies” is a perfect fit for the lonely, empty crib under the Christmas tree.

We are confident that Jesus won’t mind. This year he is simply presenting in a different form and could even entice our younger generation to draw closer to the story, seeing baby Jesus as ”one of theirs.”

Co-senior drives me to my Christmas Eve hairdressing appointment. I need him today as for some reason my car is leaking. El Nino has come to visit this Christmas. We are coping in the wet; my hair and my car are not.

He patiently camps outside the Op shop next to the hairdresser, and there, nestled amongst pinecones and Christmas stockings, is a hand-me-down, bright baby Jesus ready and waiting for adoption. We take him home, apologise to Baby Yoda Ooshie for the cupboard shelf that has now become his permanent home, and place baby Jesus right where he is meant to be. The missing angels will still be gazing down from their elusive invisible hiding place, but baby Jesus will simply remain right where he is, glowing brightly from his crib in the family hearth, heart and home.

JUST A THOUGHT

"For God so loved the world that He gave His only begotten Son, that whoever believes in Him should not perish but have everlasting life."

– Jesus Christ, John 3:16

SENIOR SAGE

I believe there is a Heaven above. It makes me feel safe in my earthly life. Are you just living for the moment or do you believe that there is something more? Is there something out there so magnificent that its presence gives even non-believers something to believe in?

Retirement

RETIREMENT IS EXCITING FOR SOME AND A HOUSE OF adjustment for others.

Some move to over "fifty-five" resorts and have never been busier.
Some remain between familiar walls, not wanting to leave a lifetime of memories behind.
Some disappear from the world, abject in their loneliness.
Some crave some space in their day.
Some crave some fun in their space.
Some remain blanketed between wake and sleep and the drone of a daytime soap.
Some buy their first activewear and cycle off to find their horizon.
Some never leave home and never drive, relying on others to check in to see if they still breathe.
Some fly off to foreign countries, desperate to keep learning and enjoy what makes them happy.
Some have the time for the first time to meet and make new friends.

Some don't want any new friends, as they can't remember the names of their old ones.
Some laugh more.
Some cry more.
Some reinvent and discover themselves.
Some wilt and drink and lose themselves.

We all crave to remain independent.
We all want to be "present".
We all worry about our finances.
We all worry about our health.
We all want to claim our happiness and barricade our choices.
We all want love.
We don't neglect living and still want to have fun.
We will never admit to being vulnerable.
We worry.
We wait.
We breathe.
We all hang on for dear life.
We live this day as if it is our last.
It might be.
We die.

And in a hundred years' time, a world full of new people start the cycle all over again.

So…

Find *your* most authentic life, *your* most authentic self, and *your* most authentic story.

Be at peace with yourself and others.

It is your story, your very own masterpiece.

Make it matter.

JUST A THOUGHT

"A retired husband is often a wife's full-time job."

– Ella Harris

SENIOR SAGE

Retirement is a major adjustment, and we oldies have time to plan and decide what direction we would like to take. Forced retirement, even though temporary, is not easy. Let us love our younger ones who are halted too soon and share our time to help out where we can.

DID I DO GOOD?

When I reach this senior stage of life,
I ask myself just one question:
Did I do good?

Acknowledgments

THANK YOU TO MY DARYL, MY CO-SENIOR, WHO HAS once again walked the walk with me both day and night. Thank you for being my coffee provider, keeping me awake in all-nighters communicating with East Coast USA while in Sydney. Thank you for picking up the pieces of the necessary daily grind that I had to ignore.

Thank you to my beta readers who are honest and brave enough to say exactly what they feel, delivering their suggestions and thoughts so very gently. It has made this story so much stronger.

To my children and grandchildren, I love you all. I know you are enjoying watching your mumma growing her wings and loving to fly.

Thank you to all the many podcasts that have included me as their guest and to all events that have invited me to be their guest speaker. It has made me more courageous in believing I can do this.

It has strengthened my resolve that at the end of the day, if I have changed one person's life for the better, then it is one more than yesterday.

www.imnowcalledasenior.com
https://www.instagram.com/imnowcalledasenior/
https://www.facebook.com/imnowcalledasenior/

Endnotes

1 Francesca Gino, *Rebel Talent: Why it pays to break the rules at work and in life* (New York: William Morrow, 2020).

2 "How Meditation Builds Healthy Hearts, Bypasses Surgery," EOC Institute, accessed 13 March, 2021, https://eocinstitute.org/meditation/key-study-shows-how-meditation-helps-heart-bypass-surgery-patients, emphasis original.

3 "Anzac Day history," Australian Government: Department of Veteran Affairs, updated 23 January, 2020, https://www.dva.gov.au/recognition/commemorating-all-who-served/commemorative-services/anzac-day-history.

4 Lea Winerman, "A healthy mind, a longer life," American Psychological Association, November 2006, Vol 37, No. 10 https://www.apa.org/monitor/nov06/healthy.

5 Martin J. Rees, *Just Six Numbers* (London: Weidenfield & Nicolson, 2015), 2.

About the Author

JULIE SURSOK IS AN INSPIRING BEST-SELLING AUTHOR of *I'm Now Called a Senior WTF.* A motivational speaker, she passionately inspires others to stand tall and feel relevant again with laughter, humility and her own life experiences.

Julie is a senior herself, a wife, mother and grandmother. She has run her own successful businesses, performed on stage and television and is an award-winning recording artist.

She emigrated from South Africa to Australia mastering the challenges of losing everything to rise back up again. Now in *I'm Now Called a Senior-Stories from the Heart,* she encourages ***you*** to reinvent and rediscover your very own purposeful life.

She lives in Sydney with her husband Daryl.

Keep up to date with what she's doing

www.imnowcalledasenior.com
https://www.instagram.com/imnowcalledasenior/
https://www.facebook.com/imnowcalledasenior/

Thank you so much for reading

I really appreciate all your feedback and I
love hearing what you have to say
If you enjoyed reading I'm Now Called a
Senior – Stories from the Heart, a review on Amazon
is always very well received and appreciated.
Thank you so much

Julie Sursok
https://www.amazon.com/dp/B087BS963W
https://www.amazon.com.au/dp/B087BS963W

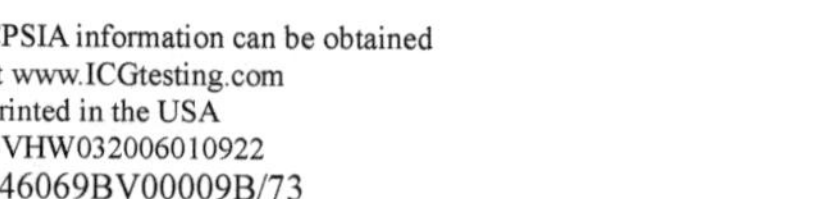

CPSIA information can be obtained
at www.ICGtesting.com
Printed in the USA
BVHW032006010922
646069BV00009B/73

9 780648 759843